Dîvân-i Kebîr

Bahr-i Hezec Ahrab Museddes

Volume 13

Mevlânâ Celâleddîn Rumi

Ministry of Culture Publications of the Republic of Turkey/2357

Dîvân-i Kebîr

Volume 13
Bahr-i Hezec Ahrab Museddes

Mevlânâ Celâleddîn Rumi

translated by
Nevit Oğuz Ergin

Echo Publications
Los Angeles, California USA

Dîvân-i Kebîr

ISBN: 1-887991-15-8

First Printing 2001
in the United States of America
in a joint publication
by

Turkish Republic
Ministry of Culture

ISBN: 975-17-1505-9 (set)
975-17-2335-3

&

Echo Publishing
Los Angeles, California, USA

Introduction

Humanity is currently stepping on the two-thousand-year mark, bringing with it thousands of years of suffering. After all these years, humans long for peace, love and tolerance. Yet, wars and conflicts still continue in various parts all over the world. While searching to solve the mysteries of space, human beings are unable to understand the secrets of peace and happiness. Man never learns his lessons of the past and because of this, he repeats the same mistakes.

Humanity needs to open a new chapter in this new millennium, no longer carrying its animosities, ugliness, and evils to the lives of our children and grandchildren.

For seven hundred years, Mevlana, a great Turkish thinker and Sultan of Heart, has been calling humanity constantly to love, friendship, and peace. He teaches us that the primary requisite for tolerance is to see people as human beings and not notice their race, religion or sect. The essence of Mevlana's philosophy is based on this kind of human love.

Reading Mevlana will help reawaken the feelings of love and tolerance within each of us. An aspiration for a world filled with peace, brotherhood, and friendship in our hearts will be more attainable with Mevlana's love.

M. Istemihan Talay
Minister of Culture
Republic of Turkey

Acknowledgments

My sincere gratitude goes to
Ms. Millicent Alexander, Ms. Mary Cuizon, and
the Ministry of Culture of Turkey
for their continued support.

Translator's Note

Among all of their adversaries, humans are probably their own worst enemy. Maybe the answers to humanity's problems are beyond humanity. Maybe beyond is where we need to go.

Mevlana began as a human being, but transcended his human nature to become close to the Almighty. He relates his journey so eloquently that once we start listening to him, we realize we don't need anything else.

We have come a long way with our translations of this magnificent work. Although ten volumes are yet to be published, the work of translation is almost complete.

You will note that we have entitled this volume Volume 13, and it is comprised of the first half of Meter 13. Among the gazels in this first half of Meter 13, there are three -- Gazel 7, Gazel 50, and Gazel 55 -- in the Murabbe, or quatrain, form. In this form, two verses make up one quatrain.

I lost my dearest friend, my biggest helper, Mrs. Terry Peart, this past year. She will always be remembered by anyone who ever reads the *Dîvân*.

Nevit O. Ergin

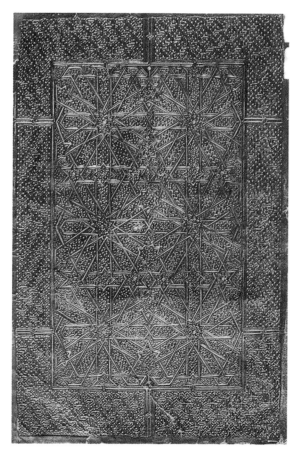

Leather binding of Dîvân-i Kebîr (c.1368)
registered at the Mevlânâ Museum in Konya, Turkey.

Dîvân-i Kebîr
Volume 13
Bahr-i Hezec Ahrab Museddes

Mefûlü Mefailün Feifün

1.

Verse 1

Page 1 of original Divan, Volume II.

Beloved, you are the only one in our heart.
The others are brick, stone and rock.

Every lover has chosen one beloved.
We haven't seen anyone but you, O beloved.

If there is another moon besides you,
Our eyes don't see it.
We are not jealous of anybody but you.

O people, as long as you don't mention Him
You may have all the beauties.

The one who has seen greatness
Doesn't bother love's play with temporary beauty.

The one who expects God's favor
Doesn't give his heart to anything but that favor.

If you would be jealous, be jealous of God.
The prophets have this jealousy, too.

What would Jesus do with churches
When He ascends to the fourth layer of sky?

Abu Bekir and Omer have chosen
Osman and Murtaza Ali.[1]

O Shems of Tebriz, let the river flow
So that the millstone will turn.

2.

Verse 11

O Soul, O One who is the cause
Of all souls becoming souls,
O One who gives wing to souls
And makes them fly!

Why would we be afraid of loss
When we are with You,
O One who turns loss into gain?

Cry help from the arrows of sight,
Help from the brows that resemble a bow.

You give sugar to ruby-lipped beauties
Whose mouths stay open with greed.

O One who puts the key in our hand,
Then makes us open the door of the world!

If you are not among us,
Why have these waists been fastened like this?

If you don't have wine whose trace doesn't appear,
What do these traces prove?

If you are created out of our illusion,
Why are these illusions so alive?
And made live by whom?

3

If you are hidden from our world,
Who brings these hidden ones into the open?

Never mind all this world's tales.
We are tired of them.

The soul who has fallen in love
With the beauty who scatters sugar
Doesn't care for heaven, won't fit there.

The one who became dust under your feet
Doesn't look for the sky.

Close my mouth with your protection.
Don't let me fall in these words.

3.

Verse 24

O one who is seriously involved with magic
And shows the gazelle like a lion to the eyes,

Eyes become cross-eyed with your spell.
You make eyes see double.

You showed an orange as a plum.
Yet, how could an orange become a plum?

Your spell showed a goat as a wolf,
Wheat as barley.

Your spell showed the roll of imagination
As the decree of immortality.

The beard of the ignorant deviate is filled
By the wind of right direction with your spell.

Your spell, O one who shows
An Indian as a Turk, made us a sophist.[2]

Your spell shows an elephant as strong as Rustem[3]
To be like a mosquito in time of war.

They fight, and their order of fate
Takes its proper course.

Don't be a sophist, be silent.
Use your divine language.

4.

Verse 34

He saw Shemseddin, who is the praise of Tebriz
And envied by China, from a distance.

He saw from a distance the eyes of that sky,
The One who gives life to the earth.

The soul who sees him in such a way
Becomes like that, even worse.

He said to me, "I'll kill you by making you cry.
I answered him, "Your ordinary servant?"

During this conversation he suddenly appeared
From the land of absence, from ambush.

He spread fire to his servant's existence,
Removed arrogance and grudges from their roots.

It was not only the tulip whose heart was burned
By that wine. The jasmine also became drunk.

Our wishes are in his shirt,
But he is shaking his sleeve at us.

He is such a sultan
That when he shows his face to the moon,
The sky puts a saddle on its horse and runs.

Sit crooked but talk straight.[4] There is
No peer to that real sultan of soul.

By God, even the auspicious Archangel
Gabriel has no news from him.

What nonsense do you talk?
He made even seven layers of sky talk.

If we open our Soul's eye and see Him,
We won't even buy Yakin[5]
For the price of one grain of barley.

Alas! That kingdom of union
Has worn the reverse side of his fur.

O love musician of my Shemseddin,
For the sake of your soul, say this:

If I don't get the chance to kiss his hand,
I'll keep my forehead on the ground.

5.

Verse 50

The moon face has shown his loyalty here.
We should never leave here.

There is help for spiritual living and pleasure
For both eyes here.

Our feet get stuck in the mud here.
How can we free our feet from here?

I swear to God that we love it here.
My God, don't exile us from here.

There is no road to death from here.
Death is to leave here.

You were borne here, like the sun.
You enlightened us here.

The soul becomes happy here;
Rejuvenates and finds immortality here.

Lift the curtain once more.
Rise once more from here.

Divine wine is here.
The cupbearer pours that wine here.

That is the fountain of life.
The water carrier
Fills your leather container here.

Hearts have found arms and wings here.
Here, mind went up in the air.

6.

Verse 61

Get up! Prepare the morning wine.
Fill our arms with musk and ambergris.

O beautiful-faced cupbearer,
Bring that colorful wine.

He asked me, "What kind of cupbearer is he?"
He is hundreds of pounds of sugar,
Halvah after halvah.

Pour the cup of wine on the head of anxiety
Which worries about every impossibility.

It is such a wine that if a sparrow drinks it,
He will get the urge to hunt the phoenix.

Before you get heavy,
Jump, come to us.

Turn around like the moon. Illuminate.
Give that red wine to the red-faced one.

Make us drunk. We will clap our hands.
Then watch us.

Watch the turning of drunks,
Their coyness. Hear their noises.

This one put his arms around the other's neck
Saying, "O my sultan, my beloved, my master."

He brought his rose face,
Kissing his beloved's hands and feet.

That one opened his face with generosity,
Saying, "Turn. Turn freely."

The other threw his mantle and turban
Saying, "Pawn them tomorrow."

The love which overflows there is more than the love
Of hundreds of mothers and fathers.

This one sees that other one as a relative.
With drunkenness, even enemies become like this.

Earthly wine causes fights. There is
No argument at God's assembly.

There is no temper, no vomiting,
No fighting there, only the cupbearer
And the wine which adorn the assembly.

Be silent so that even the infidel self says
Out of his jealousy,
"There is nobody but Him to be worshipped,"

7.

Verse 79[6]

*H*ow long will you be going backwards?
Come forward. Don't stay at heresy.
It's time to come to faith and religion.

See poison as sherbet. Grab the poison.
At last, come to the source of your source.

****

You are on earth with form. But you
Are the threat of the pearl of certainty.

You became the custodian
Of the storage of God's grace;
At last come to the source of your source.

****

If you give yourself to ecstasy,
It is sure that you will be saved from yourself.

You jumped out of the bonds of thousands of traps;
At last come to the source of your source.

****

You came from the sperm of a prince.
Open your eyes to this ordinary world.

13

Pity how joyful you are.
At last, come to the source of your source.

****

Although you are the spell of earth,
You are mine inside.

Open both your eyes.
At last, come to the source of your source.

****

You are the son of light and greatness;
Have an auspicious fate and good fortune.

How long will you be crying for illusionary things?
At last, come to the source of your source.

****

You are a ruby, hidden around hard rocks.
How long will you be deceiving us?

O my friend, he appears to your eyes openly.
At last, come to the source of your source.

****

You come like that,
Your beautiful eyes full of fire and drunk.

From the arms of the unruly beloved.
At last, come to the source of your source.

****

Shems of Tebriz, that cupbearer is offering you
A glass full of the wine of immortality;
It is pure and clear.

"Glory be to God."
At last, come to the source of your source.

8.

Verse 97

How come you leave our house with our fire,
Our flame and go to your own house?

Don't ever talk about our horse, our whip
To Rustem-i Zal,[7]

Because nothing but the truth
Will know of our cheating and deceit.

We cannot fit in anyone's heart
Because our comb is in His hair.

Wherever you see the hair of His arrow,
Make sure that our trace is there.

Talk about love. Say, "Love is a trap,"
But never mention our bait.

O heart's confidant,
Don't ever remember our story.

If you don't talk, you'll get used to it
And become mute.

There was our so and so who was the owner
Of such and such's heart at Tebriz.

9.

Verse 106

J saw that face which resembles a rose garden.
I saw the eyes of that brilliance.
I saw His light.

I saw that soul's kible,
The place for the soul to prostrate,
That joy and pleasure.
I saw that land of security.

Heart wanted to sacrifice
His soul, his self there.

Soul also started to turn
And clap his hands.

Reason came and said, "How can you talk
And praise this auspicious fortune?"

This is such a rose smell
That it will straighten up
Every bent neck like a cypress.

Everything changes with love.
Armenian becomes Turk.

O soul, you have reached the soul of souls. O body,
You have been melted, been changed from flesh.

The alms of our beloved
Make the money of the rich scarce.

Troubled Mary finds
Fresh, wet dates.[8]

Don't be too generous with the people
So that the stranger doesn't get jealous.

If the purpose of faith is confidence,
Look for confidence in solitude.

Whose land of solitude is in this heart's land?
Make it a habit to stay in the heart.

They keep serving this glass
Of immortality in the heart's house.

Be silent. Acquire the talent of keeping silent.
Quit the world full of talent.

Keep faith in your heart
Because heart is the house of faith.

10.

Verse 122

𝕴 saw a beautiful face,
A beautiful Sultan,
That eye, the light of hearts.

I saw that friend of heart, the one
Who makes my trouble his trouble,
That soul, the one who adds
Soul to souls, that universe.

I saw the one who gives mind to mind
And joy to joy.

Page 3 of original Divan, Volume II.

I saw the place of prostration
Of that moon, that sky;
I saw the one who became kible to the saints.

Every particle of mine
Was thanking God.

When Moses saw the light
From the tree,

Moses said, "Since I am saved from searching,
I have found such a gift."

God said, "O Moses, stop your journey.
Throw the staff from your hand.

At that moment, Moses threw out relatives,
Friends, neighbors, everybody from his heart.

"Take off your shoes, O Moses," ordered God.
What He meant by this was,
"Quit these two worlds which adored the heart.

"Nothing would fit in the house of heart."
Only heart knows the jealousy of the prophets.

"O Moses," God said, "what do you have in hand?"
"The staff I need on the journey," answered Moses.

"Throw that staff out of your hand
And see the marvels of the sky," He said.

He threw out the staff; it turned into a dragon.
When Moses saw the dragon, he ran away.

God said, "Grab that. Grab it
And I will turn it into a staff again.

"I will help your enemy.
I turn your supporters against you like that.

"That way, you will know that all your
Faithful friends are my gift.
No one else would be able to help you.

"If I give trouble to hands and feet
Your hands and feet will turn into a snake."

O hand, don't hang on anybody but me.
O foot, don't want to go anywhere but the place
That will be walked eventually.

Don't run away from our troubles.
There are troubles everywhere,
But those troubles are also ways to the remedy.

There isn't anybody
Who tries to escape from trouble
Who doesn't find worse trouble instead.

Stay away from bait. That's where the fear is.
O neighbor, leave fear to reason.

Shems of Tebriz did a favor,
But when he left, he took all favors away.

11.

Verse 144

Cupbearer, serve that absolute wine.
That wine which leaves no trace
Becomes a sign to His name and fame.

Keep serving. You are adding soul
To our soul. Make us drunk.
Take away our soul.

Once more come inside
Through that door that teaches cupbearers
To become the best.

Come like a spring from the heart of rock
And break the jar of flesh and soul.

Give joy to the ones
Who are in love with wine.
Give separation to the ones
Who ask for bread.

Bread is the builder of body's jail,
But wine is a rain that rains
To the garden of soul.

I covered the table of earth,
Opened the top of sky's jar.

Close your eyes which see fault.
Open your eyes that see absence.

Open them so that neither mosque
Nor idol house remains.
We wouldn't recognize either one.

Be silent. The world of silence
Fills this world with sound.

12.

Verse 154

*Y*ou said you found other friends instead of us.
Don't say that. This is impossible.

Take care of us. Don't give excuses.
Give today. Don't put us off until tomorrow.

O date tree, let me sleep
Under your shade.

O love, you mixed with my heart
Like sugar and honey are mixed in halvah.

O one whose shape, in my eye,
Resembles a pearl in that sea!

You also have our head.
Shake your head and say,
"What a nice journey."

Remember, last night you made a promise.
But, how could I dare ask you?
Where is that power?

Even I can't touch the sun.
You are my sun.
At least appear to me from a distance.

This and a thousand other suns
Are longing for you,
Asking for you.

13.

Verse 163

$\mathcal{D}$ on't make those no good ones insolent.
Don't pay attention to those common people.

When the thief-tailor finds an opportunity,
He steals material from the right-size garment.

Leave them outside the door like a doorknob.
They don't even deserve that.

They come to you as a joke, clowning.
Don't cover the obvious by expecting something.

They, themselves, are full of trouble.
How could they expel sorrow and trouble from you?

There is no cure for sorrow and grief
But the solitude of love.

Either to see the beloved or to smell his air,
What else is there in this world?

Soul would see His image
And prostrate until he sees the beloved.

Stand at His temple like a candlestick
Because there would be a chance for the great ones.

You became helpless in the present time.
When will you be able to see the essence of time?

When the eye gives up space,
It will easily see the origin of space.

Soul resembles the meal. Body is the kettle.
Put the kettle on the fire.

Put it on the fire and watch the boiling deep inside.
After that, you won't believe in stories.

You will watch the time in which you are.
The spectacle of truth is accomplished inwardly.

This is the beginning of this road.
I will show the way to lost ones.

There are some
Who have gone hundreds of stages beyond.
How can I tell this to them?

The purpose of these words is to tell you,
"You are saved. You have found the One
Who is the light of heaven."

You have reached My temple,
God's and faith's Shems;
It is the one where human and djinn take refuge.

Tebriz has turned into sky for His help.
I wish the ladder of heart would always remain.

27

14.

Verse 182

W here is that quick, learned love's musician
That would strike the plectrum with love
Rather then the wish of this one or that one?

I've had this hope with every breath
But have never seen it.
I'll go to the grave with that desire.

If you've already seen it,
How lucky for you, my dear friend. How lucky.

If he is as cancealed as Hizir is
Or he is at the sea coast,

O wind, bring our greetings to Him and explain
That we are quarreling with Him in our heart.

I know that greetings like this
Bring the Beloved to lovers.

Love is what makes the sky turn around,
Not water. We walk with love, not with feet.

The wheel of soul also turns with tears
When the name of the Beloved is mentioned.

The lasso of the Beloved's union
Is to recall Him. Be silent.
Love has become exuberant again.

15.

There is a journey for us without us.
A joy came to our heart there, without us.

That moon who has been hiding from us
Put his cheek to ours, without us.

We gave our life with his sorrow. Then his
Sorrow brought us back to life, without us.

We are the ones
Who are continuously drunk without wine.
We are the ones who rejoice, without us.

Don't even think about us.
We are the ones
Who have gone like the wind, without us.

When we are without us, we want to stay
That way all the time, without us.

All the doors used to be closed in our face;
Once he let us go without us,
All the door were opened.

Even the hearts of Keykubad are slaves
And servants for us, because Keykubad[9]
Is also a servant and slave, without us.

We are the ones who run away from good and evil,
Run away from worship and defeatism.

16.

D on't break the heart of the one
Who became your dependent. Don't torment him.

Mercy, O heart. They don't sacrifice
Lean animals in a religious way.

I am your drunk.
Put that jewel-like wine in my hand.

Give me advice.
Make peace with those narcissus eyes.

Order the magician Indians, so they
Don't carry magic beyond the limit.

The lover has fallen into that six-cornered[10]
Dungeon. Break the door of this jail.

Come forward one moment.
Gather the fairies together.

In hundreds of places, sugar bales
Have tied their belts like pencils.
It looks like they've set an army.

O love, come close like a brother.
Quit saluting like a vagabond.

O soul's cupbearer, protect the right
Of the brotherhood at God's door.

O Noah of time,
Move this anchored nature's boat.

O regent of Mustafa,[11]
Turn that big Kevser's[12] cup.

O standard bearer who is dressed in red,
Open the lip of prophecy.

Fill this field
Where everything is yellow and pale like saffron
With red roses and tulips.

I won't whiten that pearl-scattered
Red wine anymore.

17.

O my Beauty, to whom I cry
And wail all night long, saying,
"O my God, my God!"

Whether the sky cries or smiles, that is
The result of the pulling from earth.

How long has the sky kept crying to the world
And the earth been cleansed and beautified?

Hundreds of gardens and meadows
Have been adorned with smiles
From the tears of the sky.

Last night I was crying. The sky was crying.
The sky and I have the same sect, the same way.

What would come out of the tears of the sky?
Roses and fresh violets.

What would come from the tears of lovers?
Hundreds of loves and mercy
From that sugar-lipped beauty.

The eye would be closed and cry
In order to have the beloved
Show coyness with his dimples.

This tear from the cloud mixes
With the smile of earth
Just for you and for me.

Our cry and smile are all
For reaching to the end.

Be silent. When you wish something
Or desire the whole world,
Just keep on watching.

18.

Verse 226

$\mathcal{A}$s long as the beloved's image is with us,
We are in joy and witnessing a spectacle.

The hall of the house turns into a valley
When we join our friends.

When we reach our heart's desire,
Even a thorn is better than thousands of dates.

If we sleep at the quarter of the beloved,
Our cover and our mattress
Will be the star of Pleiades.

When we touch the beloved's hair,
We are in the night of Kadir.[13]
Goodness and majesty are with us.

When the reflection of your face shines,
The mountain and valley
Turn into silk, become satin.

When we ask for His smell from the wind,
The sound of the harp comes.
The sound of the shrill pipe is heard.

If we write His name on the ground,
Every piece of dirt becomes a houri.
Earth changes to heaven.

If we read his charm to the fire,
The fire melts, turns into water.

Why should we extend the story?
If we read His name,
Absence would become Existence.

The word that has a secret sign of his love inside
Has more substance
Than hundreds of thousands of walnuts.

But when love shows its face,
All of these disappear.

Be silent.
Words are depleted, finished.
Great God is the only intention and desire.

19.

Verse 239

There is a beauty in your town.
Mind and heart are restless because of him.

Everybody has his own share from him.
There is a spring in every garden from him.

There is a yell in every corner because of him.
Dust is raised on every road because of him.

There is a melody in every ear,
There is an example in every eye from Him.

O hard workers, get an early start.
A big job ahead is of us.

Secretly, a friend said in my ear,
"There is a beautiful beloved hidden here."

It is understood from the way he talks.
There is also a weak-hearted lover here.

He is the one who sends.
He is the one who is sent.
That sultan talks like that. That is his custom.

He is Noah. He saves the one
Who goes to the bottom. He is soul,
Concealed, but sometimes obvious.

Don't turn around the sour faces anymore.
There is someone next to you who scatters sugar.

Don't turn around those sugar faces too much,
Because that passion is also temporary.

There is sweetness here that has no end.
There is a time here that never passes.

Be silent, O heart. Don't think
There is a border or limit for Him.

20.

Verse 252

Today a new insanity has come in such a way
That it drags the chains of hundreds of hearts.

Today, sacks have been torn
From the bales of sugar cane.

Again, that Bedouin has bought the Joseph of Beauty
And put him inside of his heart.

Page 5 of original Divan, Volume II.

All night long, souls have grazed
With grace and charm
On narcissus and jasmine.

In the end, every soul has become agile
Because of spring
And started jumping all over.

Today, violets and tulips have grown
From stones and bricks.

Trees have blossomed in winter;
Fruits are harvested in the middle of January.

It looks like God has created
A new world in the old world.

O loving sage, read that gazel that starts,
"Love chooses you from among the lovers,"

And continues, "There is a mark
On your pale, golden face.
Maybe your silver-bodied beloved
Has bitten it."

It is possible that he may calm
This trembling heart with his sorrow.

Be silent. Visit the garden and meadow.
Go on an excursion. Today is the day
That you need your eyes.

21.

Verse 264

*A*nyone who has a donkey in his barn
Thinks he has a guide to see around the world.

The bazaar of this world stands for profit.
That's why everybody is in deep trouble.

This toil and fatigue
Pulls people to evil and bitterness.

The shell that contains a pearl
Stays in the sea.

The shell that doesn't have a pearl
Will try to find a way to search for pearls.

Sometimes in the sea, sometimes close to shore,
He keeps looking for that pearl.

Be silent. Don't look for peace and comfort.
Only the one who has a messenger
Will find peace, reach comfort.

22.

Verse 271

O one who is checkmated by love's sultan,
Don't get angry. Don't talk back.

Look at the garden of absence, then watch
The paradises of your existing soul.

If you go beyond a little bit from your being,
You will see the heavens behind.

You will see the Sultan of truth and meaning;
He has a tent made of light
That has no beginning of the beginning.

When He appears to your eye, don't look for
A miracle. Miracles are good only to find the path.

The torrent goes down to the sea coast,
But when it merges with the ocean,
Alas, no torrent remains.

O Shems of Tebriz, we are checkmated by you.
Hundreds of reverences,
Hundreds greetings from us to you.

23.

Verse 278

𝔐ake sure that time is nothing
But one kind of love.
Although our shape is beyond time.

Because this thing you call time resembles a cage.
Kafdag and the phoenix are beyond the cage.

The world is like a river. We are out of this river.
Our shadow is reflected there.

Here is the most complex, difficult metaphor.
It is not here, but it is still here.

O soul, don't smile to any face but the face of soul;
If it is not here, all smiles are nothing but crying.

The heart which is squeezed is not a heart,
Because it is very large, has no beginning, no end.

Heart doesn't worry.
Worry is not food for the heart.
It is such a parrot that it eats sugar.

Make your head like feet as the tree does,
Because your journey has ups and downs.

The branch looks at the roots
Because the power of his essence comes from the feet.

24.

Verse 287

The smoke that comes out of our heart
Is the sign of love;
That smoke from the heart is very obvious.

Blood has been boiling and foaming
In the heart, wave by wave.
This is not heart; this must be ocean.

All our friends became strangers. Even heart
Started acting like an enemy. I don't know why.

Wherever love has unloaded its load,
That is where condemnation is.

But we are not afraid of that criticism.
We have made criticism our home for a long time.

Even sultans are jealous of love,
Because love is the light of hearts.

Step to the top of seven layers of heaven,
Because love is on high levels.

Don't be sober at the assembly of love,
Because the one who is sober
Is outrageous and disgraceful there.

Don't ask to become the head here,
Because the head of the assembly
Sees even when he closes his eyes.

Love is in the tent, yet watch
The dust his army has raised.

He is behind the seven curtains,
But his grace and beauty are obvious.

O brave ones, wake up.
There is a candle. There is wine,
And the beloved is all alone.

25.

Verse 299

Ramadan came, but bairam is with us.
The lock came, but the key is with us.

Mouth is closed. Eyes are opened.
That brilliance that the eyes see is with us.

We have cleaned soul and heart with fasting.
The dirt which has been with us is cleansed now.

Some stress comes from fasting,
But the invisible treasure of heart is with us.

Ramadan came to the heart's temple;
The one who created heart is with us.

Since Salahaddin is among this crowd,
Mansur and Beyazid are with us.

26.

Verse 305

O one who loots our heart,
My soul and hundreds of others
Become prey for you.

What other kind of job do you have
Besides killing people and lovers?

You keep killing. Your hands stay healthy.
Souls of the people on earth
Are spread and scattered to You.

I have seen so many martyrs come to life
With the look of your dreamy eyes.

I have seen so many hesitants settle
In your unstable fire.

If You would kindly visit them,
No dead would remain in the ground.

Soul keeps kissing the ground where You stand
With the hope of embracing You.

27.

Verse 312

The glass of destiny is filled with poison,
But it is sweet like halvah for lovers.

What would happen if you left your place
Because of that incident?
It is all right, really; the place is there.

Don't run away from the fire of love.
Beside this fire, the rest are dust and smoke.

Smoke doesn't cook you. It only blackens.
Fire is the master of cooking you.

The moth which turns around the smoke is covered
With smoke. He is inexperienced. He is disgraced.

The one who has a journey like that in front of him
Doesn't think of either home or work.

Don't bother to go to the city. Moses is company
At the desert. Quail and manna are there.

Why do you want health? Jesus is your doctor
With every breath when you are sick.

I am content with this anxiety. When I am at ease,
Every buffoon finds space to get in my heart.

How could the house of heart be tight?
Every night that heart-catching Beloved
Is there alone.

When my heart is tight,
Nobody is able to fit there but Him.
The tightness of my heart
Is a relief from struggles for me.

The teeth of the enemy is set on edge by
Sour things;
For that reason, sour-face is salvation for us.

Be silent. The face of the sea is also sour,
But it has mines of pearls and coral.

28.

Verse 325

That hodja is very attentive,
But he is a troublemaker,
And he weighs himself too much.

I made the mistake of looking at his smile,
But become confident
When I saw him in silence.

But put your mind in your head.
There is water under the straw.
There is a rough sea under the straw.

Wherever you go, mind is the key.
But what can you do here?
Mind becomes the lock.

He looks at your face and smiles.
Don't make a mistake.
This is just a cover for his face.

Anyone who has fallen in his hand
Yells and screams like a harp.

Even souls keep turning around him
Like honey bees
Because he is the real honey.

51

He is such a lion
That sorrow runs from His majesty
And hides itself like a blind rat
In the hole of the grave.

While Shems of Tebriz is the cash of today,
Why does the world listen to the talk of yesterday?

29.

Verse 334

$\mathcal{J}$t is for the naive to waste time here.
Where do I come from?
I should find the way to go there.

To stay away from the beloved for even a breath
Is a forbidden deed in the sect of the lover.

If there is a real person in the village,
A sign is enough for him.[14]

How could the sparrow be safe
While the phoenix's feet
Are caught in this amazing trap?

O vagabond heart, don't come here.
Stay there. There is a nice stage there.

Choose that appetizer that will add soul to your soul.
Ask for that wine that is in its prime.

Beyond this,
There are all kinds of shapes, figures and colors.
Beside this, all is struggle and worry about reputation.

Be silent. Sit down because you are drunk.
Besides, you are at the edge of the roof.

30.

Verse 342

I don't eat from a boiled sheep's head; it is heavy.
I also don't eat trotter;[15] it is nothing but bone.

I don't eat roasted meat;
It is not good for your health.
I eat divine radiance. That is the food for the soul.

I don't want to be a head. Heads wear kulah.[16]
I don't want gold, because they want it back.

I don't want a donkey
Because donkeys need grass and straw.
I eat partridge, because it is the prey of sultans.

I don't fly high. I am not a stork.
I don't bite anyone. I am not a dog.

I don't limp. I am not lame.
I am in love with a beauty
As beautiful as the moon.

I don't act sour. I am not vinegar.
I don't have moisture. I am not the side of spring.

I cannot act unruly. I am not rebellious.
I am contented, because I am Mecca.

You pawned my turban.
In return, you didn't even give me a jar of boiled wine.

Be fair. You are like a bandit;
If you come to us we are full of joy.

You are the village head, the village bully.
Give me the wine you were talking about.

If you don't give it to me, expel me.
You go out and return to the place
Between your wife's inner thighs.

I eat love. It is well digested, gives pleasure
To the mouth. It is the joy of soul.

I eat a little bit of bread soaked in gravy,
A little trotter, but trotter harmed me.

From now on, we won't have anything
To do with trotter, nor with the person
Who is fond of the meal and the table.

31.

Verse 357

O one who corrects our business with his favor,
Wherever there is a cheerful place,
That is our place.

When there is a wine glass and union,
There is no worry and trouble for the lover.

Every wind which starts a new tune
Waits for our signal.

Every drop of water becomes a doorkeeper.
There is a peerless, unseen beauty behind the door.

Every drunk nightingale at the top of one sapling
Adds soul to soul, like wine.

Don't talk too much. It is time for a meal.
The hunger of the crowd has grown six times more.

32.

Verse 363

𝒥 am not saying twisted words. My mouth
Is telling secrets to your soul's ear.

Lip has been silent because of your greeting,
But His word is the same coming from your mouth.

Body is separated from You,
But soul has been holding Your skirt tightly.

In appearance, He threw you like an arrow,
But His soul is pulling you to himself like a bow.

He kept telling your soul's ear
All the things that He has hidden from you.

You are not present at this moment,
But heart grabs your belt and pulls you to His side.

In fact, He made you very close to Himself inside,
But in appearance, He keeps trying you.

Be silent. Since He gave you this sorrow;
That is the best proof
That He is pulling you to Himself.

33.

Verse 371

Someone asked, "What is your way?
I said, "This road to the abandonment
Of desire and wishes."

O one who is in love with the sultan,
Make sure your road is to look
For the consent of that great one.

If you want the Beloved's wish and desire,
Don't ask for your own wish and desire.

The Beloved's love is the suffering
Of the soul, because this love
Is the worshipping place for great ones.

His love is not less than the summit
Of the tallest mountain.
That summit is enough for us.

There is a friend of love
In the cave of that mountain.[17]
He controls the soul with his beauty.

Everything that gives you joy and pleasure
Is good. I don't determine
Which joys and pleasures they are.

Be silent. Follow the master of love.
He is Iman[18] for you in two worlds.

34.

Verse 379

*H*eart came last night and said to soul's ear,
"O beauty, the one whose name I could not repeat!"

O one who tears apart someone,
Who talks openly and burns to ashes
The one who talks secretly!

O one who tells of the trace
Of the one whose dust of his trace doesn't appear,
What kind of excuse can my soul bring?"

The only ones who know
What is going on secretly in the rose garden
Are the singing nightingale and the rose,

Not the person who listens to the sounds
Of the nightingale and makes songs out of them.

Those bow-like eyebrows have taught
The arrows of the gaze how to hunt.

Earth has spoken hundreds of different languages
To answer the questions of the sky.

Page 7 of original Diva, Volume II.

O one who falls in love with the sky,
Be a friend to the one who talks about a ladder.

Everybody mentions the house,
But where is the trace of the charmer
Who lives in the house?

The one who sits in the shade
Talks about the one who casts the shade,
But where is the gleam of the sun?

In spite of all this, a few words from that tongue
Make the ear and mind drunk.

Tongue found a couple of interruptions,
Stayed there, and left the mind.

Yet, the soul of the lover became ashamed
Of that interruption
And left the store and bazaar.

Love said in my ear, "It is enough."
I will be silent because that's what he said.

35.

My soul is in the air of the Beloved.
He keeps flying when he sees turning glasses.

His hands touch the wine.
It is such a wine
That even the sun is illuminated by its light.

When soul drinks that wine, it becomes light.
It rises up and keeps flying.

When the moon appears
And soul merges with the moon,
The sun disappears with shame.

When soul meets and is rejuvenated,
It doesn't care about or look at anyone.

36.

Verse 398

J would mention your sweet words,
Indulge in the stories
Of the source of life's fountain.

Put your cheek to my cheek so I can tell you
Why the sultan has checkmated you.

He burned your harvest,
But gave you alms from His own harvest.

In order to prevent you from talking nonsense,
He makes your cress field entirely green.

Be happy like Abraham in the fire of love
So He will save you.

Your mind has seen hundreds of Kadir's nights,[20]
Hundreds of bairams.
Your berat[21] is given with love.

I pledge your pleasant image.
I don't take an oath for your essence.

When souls are submerged in your attributes,
How can they reach your essence?

In order to purify you from your sins,
He made you flow like a river,
Made you prostrate.

In order to pull you to the land of absence,
He gave you trouble from every direction in this world.

You keep telling yourself to be silent,
But you haven't been. Even love
Is laughing at you for dragging your feet.

37.

Verse 409

I am such a lover that I gave up the road
And everything that exists in the road,
Because the companion of the lover
Is that exalted one person
Who has no beginning of the beginning.

The one whose friend is soul's God
Is not afraid of the separation of soul.

He is on a journey but, like the moon,
He settles down at a beautiful, bright face.

The one who is lighter than the wind
Doesn't wait for wind.

Love and the lover are all one.
Don't even think *two*.

When the lover and love are merged,
He gives a blessing to himself.
At the same time he, himself, is the blessing.

When he asks for this kind of order,
He turns into leather in front of Suheyl.[22]

If he goes to the sea with that desire,
Even though he is an orphan,
He turns into a pearl.

O one who has seen the kindness
And favor of Shems of Tebriz,
Don't call Hatem[23] the most generous.

38.

While the nightingales are singing,
  The rest of the birds keep silent.

Furthermore, they don't have a harvest.
Haven't they eaten grain
Fom the harvest of absence?

Those sultans are ring stones.
But we are also in the circle of the ring.

If they don't want to hear my noise,
Why did they create me?

That sultan desires sweet as well as sour;
That's why they put two kettles on the fire.

Sour is also necessary in the kitchen
Because half-drunks are fond of that.

Every state of us is a nutrient for a group.
Even the ones in absence grow with those foods.

Birds of heart are from heaven.
For only a few days
Their feet are tied here on earth.

They are the stars of faith.
That's why they are not tied, even to the sky.

The reason for their being on earth
Is to appreciate God's union
And suffer through separation from God.

Even if they cast parts in earth,
They don't leave them there.
They gather them.

Shems of Tebriz used to say very little.
All sultans are patient and confident.

39.

Verse 430

Cupbearer, serve more
Of that newly purchased wine.
Friends just came.

The number of guests has increased.
Give more wine from the jar
That we attained and tasted.

Give that wine whose smell
Caused Abdal[24] to become hidden
And apparent among the people.

O beautiful cupbearer, thank God
That they saw your beautiful face.

O fire which burns the lover's belongings,
Lovers have brought their belongings with your love.

O one who dropped the curtain
And went behind it! The lover
Has torn the curtain with your love.

O love, everybody is cheerful because of you.
Lovers were born from your light.

You are a sultan
And all lovers have your colors.
They are all from the sultan's descendants.

Everyone who has head and eyes
Has seen you, has put his head to the ground.

You are the sun. Particles are from you.
They give this light back to the other light.

When you help, all the Zal's
Become Rustem in the war.

But, if help doesn't come from you,
It doesn't matter if they are Hamza[25] or Rustem.
Altogether, they are the wind.

O heart, jump. The moon-faced ones
Open the curtain of absence
And show their faces.

They are all drunk. No one knows the road
To his house because they are drunk, although
Not on the wine which has set and spoiled.

As long as love lives, they also live.
As long as remembrance exists,
They will be remembered.

40.

We became drunk. Heart separated from us,
But I don't know where he ran to.

When my heart saw reason,
It broke its bonds and started to run away.

He wouldn't go just anywhere.
Maybe he went to the privacy of God.

Don't look for him at home.
He is a bird of sky. He flew.

He is the white falcon of the sultan.
He has flown toward the sultan.

41.

Verse 450

Don't talk about justice,
Punishment of the soul
That was born from the glory of Mohammed.

Fish don't try to learn to swim.
The cypress doesn't look for freedom.

The thorn that has been grown in the garden of joy
Sees the rose garden full of joy.

Page 8 of original Divan, Volume II.

The canopy of joy, the arch of pleasure
Is apart from fire, earth, water and wind.

These four simple elements which resemble a cross
May be removed from the heart
Of the brave ones who search for unity.

There is a bright sky on that side. There is a sultan
Who has set an ambush, is watching there.[26]

His casual looks give two eyes to people.
He has divine sight, divine wisdom.
He is the Pir[27] Master.

If you looked at this world of mud
With the eye of soul,

You would see that every corner
Is filled with light like the night of creation,
But nobody is able to see that.

There are thousands of suns in each cloud.
Every ruin is turned into heaven.

You will put your throne
At the house of the attained ones,
Raise your tent over the poles.

You will get the smell from Shems of Tebriz,
To whom even the angels submit and yield.

42.

Verse 462

Night has gone. O friends, where are you?
When night has passed, come over.

Come and drink wine from ruby lips,
Eat sugar from smiles.

When morning comes,
Show the effects of that wine to sober ones.

Since they blew on your bosom,
If you deliver,
You may as well deliver Jesus.

Rise like the full moon,
Without eight heavens and seven hells.

If you still have a thought even as small as a hair
About seven and eight,
You don't deserve this private union.

Hair in the eye is not a simple matter.
Put a salve on it immediately.

When the eye is cleansed from hair
You become a guide to love, like the eye.

Be fair. No self is left in you
Because you become such a Self
With the love of the master of masters,
Shems of Tebriz.

43.

Verse 471

It is a shame to be wary,
To be concerned at the place
Where a beautiful someone like you stays.

When mercy, that has no boundary,
Becomes exuberant,
Fright and worry are withdrawn to a corner.

I have stolen a kiss by force.
My friend, force is counted only three times.

Show tolerance to the third one today.
One kiss will be counted as a thousand today.

I am water. You are the riverbed.
Water naturally kisses the riverbed.

When water kisses the riverbed,
Flowers blossom and grass grows.

What will the meadow be missing
If confused man's eye sees grass as thorns?

Why is Moses afraid of the staff?
Because the staff became a snake
Only in front of the pharaoh.

The Nile became blood for the one who followed
The pharaoh, but sweet water for the believer.

Abraham never was afraid of fire,
Yet Nimrod was burned in it.

Jacob didn't turn away from Joseph,
Even though that closeness
Bothered the other son.

That wind raises dust in barren lands,
But it is spring for gardens and meadows.

That breeze brings leaves out of branches.
Later, flowers come on top of the leaves.

O love, when Ahmed[28] is with you, isn't it a shame
That you hang around with Abu cehil?[29]

If you won this, take it.
If you lost that, too bad.
The world's affair is real gambling.

The one who tries to run away from his fate
Will run, but at the end, will fall in desperation.

Come back to your senses. Don't set a trap
For the rabbit so the lion will become prey for you.

O heart, don't talk much about Love's ambergris;
One who is friend to you is able to get its smell.

44.

That beautiful-faced Joseph has come.
That present-time Jesus has come.

A hundred thousand helps come like a flag,
Suddenly, with the parade of spring.

O one whose work is to enliven the dead,
Get up; the time has come to start work.

That lion-hunter lion has come
Like a drunk to the garden, the meadow.

Yesterday, the day before yesterday,
They were all gone. Look now. Today,
That beauty of mine has come to us
Like cash money.

Today, this town has become paradise.
"The sultan has come," it is saying.

Beat the drum. Today is bairam.
Enjoy, sing and dance. The Beloved has come.

A Moon appeared from the land of absence,
Such a moon that this moon
Became dust right on its surface.

The beauty of the beautiful one
Who gives constancy to soul
Made the whole world unstable.

All come to your senses. Open love's hand.
Presents are scattered from the ninth-level heaven.

O bizarre bird whose wings were cut,
Instead of two wings, four wings have come.

O heart that is full of anxiety, relax.
That lost friend has come to your arms.

O feet, come, enter the dance, tap on the floor.
That famous wine has come.

Don't talk about the old one. He is rejuvenated.
Don't talk about last year. Last year has arrived.

You said, "What excuse shall I bring to the sultan?"
In fact, the sultan has come with an excuse.

"How can I be saved from his hands?
Where shall I go?" you said.
His hands keep helping.

You saw fire and came like light.
You saw blood and came like wine.

Be silent. Don't count his favors.
He is a favor that cannot be counted.

45.

Verse 507

The heart that hasn't taken a silver body
Resembles a man without a head.

The person who is separated from love's trap
Is like a bird without wings.

How does the one who doesn't know
Where the news comes from
Know about the world?

The one who doesn't have a shield of love
Will surely be sacrificed to the eye's arrow.

The one who doesn't have a heart for the journey
Wouldn't know about the value of liver.

A pearl is dropped on the road;
The only one who will benefit from that
Is the one who takes the journey.

The one who doesn't turn around that pearl
Will have neither pearl nor bead.
He will not even have strength or power.

Put your mind in your head.
Go to sleep. Dawn has come,
Though our evening never ends in dawn.

46.

Verse 515[31]

O one who is the essence of every wish,
You came late.
Don't leave early.

O one who burns heart, who hurts our nose
With the fire of the intention of departure,

Every piece of aloe wood burns in fire.
Yet, to be thrown in your fire
Is like a wedding bairam for aloe wood.

Your hope says in every breath,
"With my favor I will hold your hand
In the near future."

But don't say,
"What will happen, will happen,
No use to work and struggle."

Page 9 of original Divan, Volume II.

I am not tied to woof , like warp.
Don't deprive me of my power and strength.

If I want, I will cut you down.
If I want, I will make you grow.

Close your mouth. Don't talk.
Prostrate in front of the Beloved.
He is the One to be worshipped.

O One whose blessings are innumerable,
O One whose work on His way can't be refused,

You did favors for us,
Called us to worship for You.

The One who came from His great temple
Gave the news of his union.

The promise of the beloved is very sweet.
Trying to reach the auspicious One
Is also auspicious,

Especially such an auspicious One
That would snatch hundreds of hearts
With every moment.

47.

Verse 528

Rain the pearls of devotion.
Scratch the heads of lovers now.

We became earth for you. Don't sow
The seeds of reproach and cruelty now.

Don't deem proper
This torture to the oppressed
On the road of separation.

O ones who belong to Venus,
Keep playing melodies from high and low tunes
At the roof of that door.

Keep playing so you will be wounded
By the sorrow of separation like me.
Your heart has already been wounded.

Nobody is deprived of that door.
Otherwise, you wouldn't count me as a man.

This is such a sorrow
That even a mountain
Becomes dust with that sorrow.
What can you say to pieces of particles?

O lion hunters, while hunting lions
You have become prey to that gazelle now.

Because of that lion hunter's narcissus eyes,
You became drunk
Without drinking the wine of union.

You fell in love with such a love,
Because of that rose-cheeked charmer,
That your face turned a saffron color.

There are troubles that go with that treasure.
For that, be patient.
Be persistent and loyal.

If you know your way, walk bravely
In the way of love. Be a man.

Since the lover has hundreds of lives,
Give one of them
Without fear and hesitation.

Soul doesn't become lost.
Don't be afraid. You are after the soul
Who has been attained.

O one who teaches deceit in love,
You are pledged to hundreds of gambles.

Love permits the fraud.
You are pledged to hundred of gambles.

You have the right to become a thorn
To all rose faces
With that tall cypress' love.

You also have the right to appear
As a snake to the pharaoh of Self
With the love of Moses.

Make soul like a shield for His troubles
Because you are Zulfekaar[32]
In the hand of love.

You are like Kafdag in endurance.
You are quiet and good-tempered
Like a mountain.

If that secret sea appears,
You become restless like a wave.

You resemble spring's cloud
For the time of scattering pearls.

Even if you become a martyr,
You will become one by the sultan's arrow.
Even if you become dust,
You will rise in front of the moon.

Your persistence is like the cypress.
You are new and fresh;
You have fruit like the big branches.

You are an apple in His tree.
You are stoned like an apple, like a tree.

Even if a stone-hearted one throws stones,
You are a friend of the cave
With the One in your essence.

You are like curtains at the side,
But running after Him like a skirt.

You are on the journey
With your moon-face turning constantly
Like the sky.

You are love. At the same time,
Love is you. Your halter is the same
As the camel of love.

If the self is a thief, breaks
The wall or roof, it doesn't matter.
You are in that safe, strong fort.

If you are lucky, drink the wine
From love's hand. Eat the meze[33]
From love's hand.

As you see, He is weaving and sewing You.
Why do you keep seeing images?

Since He already makes you old,
Why are you after the fight
Of force or free selection?

If you are a lover, if you have
The eye of admonition,
Accept one command, one force.

You follow me in talk or in silence.
But I would rather keep silent.

48.

Verse 563

*W*ithout your favor heart is lifeless.
Soul doesn't care for the world
Without you.

Reason has a big house, a big mansion,
But without your table,
It has no water and no bread.

The sun has seen the soul of your quarter.
Now it doesn't care for the sky.

Since the pomegranate's flower
Saw the rose garden of soul,
It forgot the garden and meadow.

What would be the harm
If the poor benefited and profited
From Your grace?

Without Your moon face,
Night is a poorly-dressed, dark-haired cloth.
It doesn't own the moon or a kingdom.
All it has is a dark, black dress.

The night has thousands of stars,
But without the moon,
It has neither light
Nor a place to put the light.

Soul has no ear without Your words.
Without Your words,
Soul has no tongue.

That bizarre soul cries, keeps begging.
Nobody interprets that,

But his pale face and tears
Are the evidence of his secret suffering.

After those two, the third witness
Is his cold deep sighs; This *Ah*
Is cold, but it has no eyes.

The essence of this cold sigh
Is heart's love. That base, that essence
Has no cold winter.

Your spring enlivens him,
Makes Him agile like the heart. Even if
A hundred thousand mountains of sorrow come,
He doesn't mind.
He puts them on his shoulder. [34]

That young, fresh love
Which resembles your spring,
In fact, rejuvenates the old ones.

How long will he be talking
About his signs and traces?
Be silent. In fact, He is the One
Who originates signs and traces,
But his sign and trace never appears.

You are also like Shems of Tebriz
Who has no boundary.
Give up sign and trace.

49.

Verse 579

The one who has color from you in his mouth,
Has a shortage of sustenance.
Be fair. Is this possible?

The one who attempts to fight with you
Fights with his dear life.

The fish that finds the water of life
Doesn't waste time on the land.

If the Kaiser of Rum is not reflected
In the mirror, you can be sure
That the mirror is rusty.

If you see a pig in your heart
That resembles Jerusalem,
You can be sure that Jerusalem
Has been conquered by the Franks.[35]

A sweet-talking beauty
Is holding us in his arms, like a harp.

This harp gives beautiful melodies
Because of his strokes.

The particle that dances with us
Doesn't care to look east of the sky.

I swear by your soul that the soul
Which limps on the way
Is afflicted with lameness.

Because this sea is full of favors,
It is impossible for crocodiles
To exist there.

The soul that becomes disobedient
Like a tiger to such a lion
Has the disposition of a dog.

While there is such a garnet,
If soul involves stone and brick,
It must be hard and useless.

Be silent. Don't look for the place
Of the word, because this place
Puts you to sleep like opium.

91

50.

Verse 592

The first look was casual, but even so,
It still wanted to obtain the source of beauty,
Reach the essence.

If love is a sin and disbelief,
Doesn't that come from that fairy after all?

****

We become colorless because of your color.
For that reason, we stay away from reason.

Rum chooses either a color or black;
Aren't they choosing from that fairy after all?

****

He walks toward the sultan's tent;
He also has an army from the brilliance of His east.

It doesn't matter if he missed the main street.
In the end, doesn't his road go to that fairy after all?

****

To fly like the moon, to run face and head down
Without wings like a shadow,

To bend down with the wind like a cypress,
Aren't they all from that fairy after all?

∗∗∗∗∗∗∗∗

His beautiful moon face which caresses Jupiter
Gives life to Azer's[36]idol.

Because of that *it*, the Samaritan made a mistake.
Whatever it is, isn't that from the fairy after all?

∗∗∗∗∗∗∗∗

O my soul, if eighteen thousand worlds
Have been filled wit my gossip, O my soul,

Either I become possible or impossible. O my soul,
Isn't the end of this from that fairy after all?

∗∗∗∗∗∗∗∗

Even if we become slim like the moon,
Still we are cheerful,
Because we are behind that sun of justice.

Even if we have an eclipse like the moon,
Isn't that because of that fairy after all?

∗∗∗∗∗∗∗∗

We quit modesty, broke the bottle of honor.
We are drunk,
Broke hundreds of vows of repentance,
Gave up hundreds of oaths,

Cut our hands instead of the tangerine.
We did it all.
Isn't that because of that fairy after all?

****

If an indiscreet one talked about that purple glass
And the source of the water of immortality

And tried to show a trace of them,
Isn't that from that fairy after all?

****

If we talk about the season
Beyond these four seasons,
If we talk about the essence of the essence
Of that spring before springtime,

If we indulge in words about His union,
Isn't that because of that fairy after all?

****

Be silent. It is impossible to talk
About the things to be talked about.
It is necessary to tell the secrets through the soul.

If this heart became drunk
And talked about His track,
Isn't it because of that fairy after all?

51.

Verse 614

The one who is not afraid
For his life isn't afraid
Of killing good or bad people.

The one who sees the beauty of Joseph
Is not afraid of the envious
And also not afraid of envy.

The one who is caught in the air
Of the sultan is not afraid
Of an army of soldiers.

Even an animal is not shy
Because of a kick,
Nor does it lash out
For the pleasure of a friendly chat.

One who feels eternal happiness
Is not afraid of immortality.

It is necessary to have a heart
Like Uhud's mountain
That is not afraid of anyone but God.

The bird that has escaped
From body's trap is not afraid
No matter where he flies.

Wherever he arrives, he is a treasure;
A martyr of the only God
Is not afraid of the grave.

The one whose essence is water
Is not afraid of water
Even if he is forcefully submerged.

The body kneaded by the soil of paradise
Is not scared
While flying over hell.

The one who is helped inside
Is not afraid of this helpless universe.

If the ignorant is unafraid of reason
It is not from his bravery;
It is from his stupidity.

The one who pulls himself
From You and Your love without fear
Has no brain.

The one who tears the curtain
Of *myself-yourself* without fear
Tears his own curtain.

The fool who hurts the heart of sultans
Without fear is a cursed one.

Since he doesn't have the antidote,
Why does he taste the world's poison
Without fear?

How could he dare look at a beauty
In the temple of those
Who see and watch?

Be careful. Make your head like feet
And walk on such a road.
Isn't your heart afraid
Of His observation there?

Money changers are on watch,
But the thief steals, unafraid.

All the wolves are shepherds there.
No one is afraid of even hundreds of people.

There, there is no me, you or he
Who borrows from himself and is not afraid.

Your heart is never afraid of you,
Is not afraid of your loose talk.

The rose garden is not afraid of spring,
Of meadow, iris or the tall cypress.

Heart has opened and grown,
Seen its own face.
From now on it is not afraid to be accepted
Nor scared of being denied.

This sea keeps giving pearls
Until the last day of judgement,
Still has more. Be silent.

52.

Verse 639

ow helpless is the one
Who has no money and no shield
From the gold mine!

How helpless is this heart without You.
It is like a parrot without sugar.

He has power, has thousands of kingdoms,
But there is something else.
Alas, he doesn't have that.

His hand that offers glasses says
That what he doesn't have,
We will give him.

If that tree doesn't have water,
We will pour the fountain of life.

For the ones who have no leaf, no branch,
We will give so many leaves
That they cannot find the green branches.

To the one who is not aware of us,
To the ones who say,
"No one hears our praying,"

We will give eyes to the ones
Who don't look at us. In fact,
The time is coming close.

Be silent. Nothing but God's hand
Can unravel the forms of soul.

53.

Verse 648

H ow helpless is the one
Who doesn't have wine.
He keeps squeezing unripe grapes.

How helpless is that barren land
Where the rain of favor and kindness
Never touch.

This time my heart is drunk in the morning
And pays its debt from the evening.

I told the one who was asleep
At the time of drinking morning wine,
"Wake up. Raise your head. I'll pay for the drinks."

Page 11 of original Divan, Volume II.

Shame has left me this day
When He would put henna in the palm[37]
Of this drunk.

There is a cupbearer today.
He has grabbed my ear.
He doesn't let me be free
For even one moment.

His staff-like glass has become a dragon
And keeps attacking the gypsy mind.

Be silent. Watch, the jar of drunks
Keep asking for wine like the glass
Whose value is so great.

54.

Verse 656

Soul has returned from a long journey,
Has reached the ground
In front of the door again.

The one who is gold
In the world of existence
Came out from the treasure of absence
In order to be cut in front of golden scissors.

Without your love, the door of heaven
Become so great
That the One who ascended to the sky
Couldn't pass through the doors of the sky.

The ones who haven't been rebellious
Towards You understood their position
And realized how worthless they were.

Soul went to do something without You
And became so frustrated
That he was unable to do anything.

He understood truly during his journey
That everything is temporary without You.

Today, he came to You
With the the road's dust
And kept begging You to be merciful.

Pull your head out of the window
So he can see
The Beauty of Taraz[38] coming.

Pull your head out of the window
So that lovers will yell,
"Kible for every Mamaz has come."

My soul which resembles a falcon
Flew out of Your temple, but when
He heard the sound of Your drum,
He returned to the temple.

O ones who are tied with strings,
You are free now.
The order for freedom has come
With his beautiful writing.

There was no sound, no breath
On that joy's harp. Start dancing.
It is playing again.

You are freed from the chain of begging
Because He, the one who
Ties thousands of coy ones, has come.

Try to leave this body's donkey
Because the one who rides Burak[39] has come.

The light of God's Shems of Tebriz' face
Covers the earth.
Secrets are spread today.

55.

Verse 671[40]

The first look was casual, but even so,
Wanted to obtain the source of Beauty,
To reach the essence.

If love is a sin and disbelief,
Doesn't that come from that fairy after all?

****

That purple wine glass,
That water of immortality,

That eye of eternity, aren't they all
From that fairy after all?

****

There are unions of happy souls
Because of that scattered hair
That is divided in half.

And their gathering at the assembly
Of that great sultan, aren't they all
Because of that fairy after all?

****

We became colorless because of
Your color. We stayed away from earth
For a thousand miles.

At that moment our souls became bewildered.
But, isn't that from that fairy after all?

****

An army has gathered in the shade
Of the sultan's tent.

My soul started to journey. Isn't that
Because of that fairy after all?

****

To bend with sorrow like a new moon,
To run with face and head like a shadow,

To hear a voice from the land of heart,
Isn't that because of that fairy?

****

That moon which burns Jupiter,
The beauty who breaks the idols of Azer!

What happens if heart chooses
To become a heretic? Isn't that
Because of that fairy after all?

****

If eighteen thousand universes
Are filled with my gossip, O my soul,

Doesn't that light which illuminates
Those universes come from His face,
O my soul? Isn't that all
From that fairy after all?

****

If we give the toll of love's road,
If we rejoice from that moon and sun,

If we open new eyes to him,
Isn't that from that fairy after all?

****

We are freed from our shame.
We drank the wine that came
From His smell and became drunk.

We broke glasses and glasses.
Aren't they all from that fairy after all?

****

The garden that has taken
A lifetime to reach
Is nicer than spring
And the four seasons of earth.

The essence of the essence of that garden
Is Shems of Tebriz. Isn't that
Because of that fairy after all?

56.

Verse 693

That flame of divine light is walking,
Swaying from side to side. That Beauty
Who become a challeng even to houris,
Is walking, swaying from side to side.

Night has put on white adorned dresses
Because that moon is walking,
Swaying from the distance.

Good news to the drunks from last night.
The cupbearer woke up for Sahur[41]
Walking, swaying.

We keep burning the soul like aloe wood,
Because that crystal mine is walking,
Swaying from side to side.

Watch this instigator
Who is walking with such exaltation,
Swaying from side to side.

That beauty who is the enemy of love's patience
Shed the blood of the patient
And plunged into that blood,
Walking and swaying from side to side.

My life is sacrificed to that Solomon.
He is walking, swaying toward the ant.

Don't look at anything
But the lover's faces,
Because that jealous sultan
Is walking and swaying side to side.

He is walking in Shems of Tebriz' body
Like the trumpet on judgment day,
Walking, swaying side to side.

57.

Verse 702

Where are you, O one who drank
The morning wine? Night is passing.
Don't do that to me.

Raise your head from the soul
Of morning wine like the shining sun.

O ones who count the evenings,
If it must be necessary to count,
You might as well count his hairs
Which resemble the night.

If you become prey to the lion,
Show me the wound in your hand.

O ones who are tired and bored,
Who fall asleep, leave this privacy to us.

Since you are waiting for that
Peerless beauty,
That peerless beauty is coming here tonight.

The reason for that is that
Shems of Tebriz knows
That you are waiting for him.

58.

Verse 709

Today, our peerless beauty didn't
Come. Our beloved, our charmer
Didn't come.

The rose that stands in the middle
Of our soul's garden
Didn't come to our arms tonight.

We should go toward the valley like a gazelle,
Because that musk of Tatar's land
Didn't come.

O spark of musician, sing that song,
"The beauty who enlightens our work
Did not come."

Don't stop playing the ney and tambourine;
Our peace and constancy
Did not come.

That cupbearer of soul didn't appear.
The remedy of our drunkenness
Didn't come.

O Shems of Tebriz, you tell it.
How come our season of spring
Hasn't come?

59.

Verse 716

𝒲 hat happened to the world last
Night because of our beauty?
What shape did the sky turn into
Because of my moon?

How was heart playing against his face?
What has happened to soul
With the fire of love?

Page 12 of original Divan, Volume II.

When eye became drunk from his looks,
What shape did mouth turn into
From his sweet lips?

What has been hunted
By his arrow-like eyelashes?
What are those bow-like eyebrows doing?

At best, he was giving color to the tulip.
Otherwise, what business did he have
In the rose garden?

What did the rose say to greenery
At that moment? Into what shape
Did the juda tree turn because of the narcissus?

For what other reason was he
Galloping in the sky
Other than to give it light?

Without his endless, limitless favor,
How could the moon stand there?

Once He looked through the land
Of absence, O my God, what shape
Did the world of existence become?

When He opened His traceless,
Shapeless curtain, what happened
To this world of trace and shape?

Night has passed and is gone.
A day has appeared without night.
What happened to this doorkeeper-like reason?

Because of Shems of Tebriz' occult gayb[42] eye,
What shape does this eye,
Which knows the unknown gayb, become?

60.

W hat does that beautiful-faced
Merchant have? What is the
Worth of his goods in our market?

He sells charms, doesn't pay attention.
Ask for his goods.
Let's see what he has.

Take his cash. Find out
How much he has
And how much is left for the robber.

What does he have of cleanliness and sweetness?
Find out if you don't have a scale to measure it.

Hold him with conversation
And find out how much
Of the wine of immortality he has.
Try to get a smell.

How lucky is the person
Who constantly searches his soul
To find out what he has,
To earn God's blessing.

What does he have in common
With the one who attained?
What does He have in common
With the Prophet's taste?
He keeps searching for that all of the time.

I said to a Kalender,[43] "Look and see:
This sky is folded down. What's wrong?"

He answered, "We don't care what
The sky has, what has happened to it."

I am drunk, quite drunk. May God help.
What help does God have?

Because of the blessings of Shems of Tebriz
There is a different thing in every heart.

61.

Verse 739

Cupbearer, get up.
That moon-faced one has come. Run,
Because He has come surprisingly.

Ride your horse like a Turk.
Time is short. Don't rest.
That Hitay Turk has entered the tent.

I wouldn't even surmise that happiness;
Look at this glory
That has come suddenly and unexpectedly.

When the wine glass roared with laughter,
The lover was filled with blood
Like a glass.

Whoever has a chance to meet
A moon like you, if he is not
In a hurry, he must be stupid.

A straw that runs away from love's harvest
Ends up in the straw barn.

Time has passed. Glory to the one
Who runs away from himself
And arrives at the threshold.

117

The one who has escaped from separation
And entered the right road at Tebriz
Shall have joy and happy pleasures.

62.

Who could tell secrets to a beloved like you
Or tell his story from the beginning?

Smart ones would tell you very briefly,
But the lover
Would keep talking and talking.

He would prostrate with Your love,
Pray with Your name in namaz.

You callously say about the words
Of my heart's pleading,
"All of these are lies."

I resemble Eyaz. You are like Mahmud.[44]
Listen to what Eyaz[45]is saying.

Somebody mentioned something
About me to you. Apparently you said,
"He always talks of frivolous things."

You hear my words of gold,
Then you say,
"He talks like scissors."

63.

Verse 754

We don't have any load in this caravan.
The ones here don't have our Beloved's fire.

There are green trees, but none of them
Has the smell from our spring.[46]

Your soul resembles the rose garden,
But your heart hasn't been
Hurt by our thorn.

Your heart is a sea of truth,
But it doesn't have our exaltation,
Our washing of the shore.

The mountain has also settled down,
But, by God, it doesn't have
Our consistency.

The soul who has become drunk
With all kinds of morning wine
Doesn't have a smell of our drunkenness.

Even the player of sky, Venus,
Doesn't have the power
To complete our work.

Ask of us God's lion. Not every
Lion can stay in our desert.

Don't show Shems of Tebriz' money
To others who are not of our rank.

64.

Verse 763

*Y*ou shouldn't do that to the one
Who wants to become your slave.

O beloved whose face is beautiful,
Whose character is charming,
Heavens would never give birth
To a pearl like you.

Since your face, your temper are beautiful,
The secret in your heart also should be beautiful.

When man dies, there is no tomorrow for him.
In a situation like that,
Why does he do cruelties today?

Why does he do things to others
That he doesn't want done to himself?

Don't crush anybody with anger,
So that God's anger won't crush you either.

Don't try to shed peoples blood,
So that same thing won't happen to you.

If apprehension doesn't come to your heart,
Fate will turn that event away from you.

O one who said, "I am dead."
What kind of death is it
That satan is possessing you?

65.

Verse 772

When will this cage change
Into a garden and meadow?
When will it become the way I expect?

When will this deadly poison turn into honey,
This terrible thorn to jasmine?

When will that half moon
Be borne in my arms? When will the envious
Be tried by grief and sorrow?

When will Egypt's Joseph invite us
By saying, "Come on in."
When will Jacob have a shirt?

When will the sun cast a shadow for us?
When will this basin
Become a house for that candle?

When will joy's harp be tuned
In a new way? When will this ear
Hear the sound of *ten-ten*?

When do we thresh grain in the moon's harvest?
When will we walk around Yemen
Like the brilliance of Suheyl.[47]

When will love's wine ferment
In the jars? When will the rebab[48]
Be played while we eat kebap?[49]

When will our desire's bird-of-luck
Come from Kafdağ
And be prey to Shibli and Abu-l Hasan?[50]

When every particle returns to the sun,
Every drop will become
The garden of Eden for generosity.

Every lamb will drink milk from the lion.
Every elephant will become
A captive of the rhinoceros.

Every corner of our town
Will turn into the land of Huten
Because of the abundance
Of charmers and moon-faced beauties.

Every lover who has been frustrated, his head dizzy,
Will be able to play love games
And reach his wishes.

Page 13 of original Divan, Volume II.

He will come back to life like a dead body.
He will give up shroud and shirt.

When will this garrulous mind
Become crazy and borrow reason
From the ear that is full of melodies?

The souls and hearts of hundreds
Of thousands of crazy and insane ones
Will kiss the Beloved and cheer up.
Their mouth and lips
Will pour honey and scatter sugar.

When will the time come
That the souls of drunks will be cupbearers
For thousands of gatherings?

The soul that laughs in love's sleeve
Will reach name and fame with love
Among men and women
And become someone of distinction.

Everyone who has fallen
Into the well of separation
Will find a rope and a way out.

Don't tell the rest of them. Keep them
In your heart. It is better to say
The words in that way.

66.

O soul's player, since you have
The tambourine, play that tune,
"Beloved, come like a drunk."

That beautiful charmer showed
His face so that even the moon
Started to worship the idol in the sky.

Particles in the world came,
Dancing from the land of absence to existence
With the love of that sun.

Why have you been grieved?
Perhaps an ogre has kept you
From the journey
And started fooling around with you.

Leave the ogre alone. Pick up the glass.
Love came to your hand
From the assembly of Elest.[51]

Play that tune. Jupiter came
From the sky to this ordinary world
To comfort the ones whose hearts
Are broken.

Keep turning around the circle
Of broken-hearted ones,
Because fortune is at the level
Of broken Hearts. So is glory.

This daily struggle,
This drink is like Namaz;
This turbid sorrow is like Abdest.[52]

Be silent. Look with silence.
Even the nightingale
Lowered himself by singing.

67.

Verse 801

What is wrong with that beautiful-faced hodja?
What pure things does he have
On his heart's mirror?

Come to your senses. Don't get into his sack.
First, ask what he has.

Make him talk. Find out if he has any smell
From the wine of immortality.
Get a smell from him.

What does he have from tulips and narcissus?
Get into his rose garden.

He is talking
About the works and tracks of the prophets.
See what he has from the essence of the prophets.

He keeps reciting prayers.
But, see if he has any cleanliness from Mustafa.

Who is he? What does he have?
What doesn't he have?
If you want to know this,
Stay with him. Stay in his shadow.

Reach your own cupbearer.
Don't even think who there is
In this three-stringed instrument.

For good omen, don't separate yourself
From that foundation.
See what this foundation has, one by one.

Don't worry about what is in front of ambergris;
Don't take this world of straw seriously.
Don't seed the wind and harvest the storm.

68.

O friend, whose torments are accepted
As loyalty, what has happened to your promise?

All mourning changes to wedding joy
When we see your face, but if we don't see You,
All wedding joy turns into mourning.

The palace becomes a ruin without Your good luck,
But ruins turn into a palace with You.

When You call, existence annihilates.
With Your separation, beings turn into nothingness.

O Charmer, who blames and kills me
Because I am pleased and content with You!

That seed in the soul is from You.
Because of You, his hand became generous.

Soul is excited from Your enrichment.
Otherwise, soul is poor and destitute.

If Your generosity were not fond of giving,
How could soul fall in love with prayer?

When the light of your cupbearer
Is reflected on the cloud,
The cloud becomes a water carrier.

When Your patience reflects on the mountain,
The mountain becomes support for the earth.[53]

Your greatness reflected to heaven,
And Your meaning appeared like the sky.

Earth also received news from Your beauty;
It became the beautiful, heart-catching Joseph.

Leave the words alone.
When you keep silent,
Your meaning becomes organized.

69.

Time's bath adds soul to soul
Because our fairy[54] is there.

Fairies have seen Him and have become bewildered.
They are talking about Him,
Telling what He has done.

Mind is the light that shows events and experiences.
Yet, there is no mind and no reason over there.

Reason is a mosquito in front of love's storm.
What strength does mind have there?

The Archangel Gabriel accompanied
The prophet Mohammed up to the Sidre[55]
And stopped there.

"Beyond that," He said, "is absolute love.
If I take one more step, I will be burned."

To extol and to reach are two opposite things.
They disintegrated in the land
That has no beginning and no end.

Man is the one who was extolling this.
He was also annihilated in Union.[56]

Leyla became Mecnun there because craziness
Is intensified a thousand times there.

Such an open-faced beauty appeared
That all the skirts of beauty
Turned into rubbish in front of him.

Joseph became Zuleyha[57] in the land of love.
There is nothing more that could be done.

The one who blew the trumpet on Judgment Day
Became lifeless.
Everything besides soul disappeared.

All these words have plunged into the sea.
It is time to swim now.

70.

Verse 837

W hy are you grieved and sorrowed?
The time for travel has come.
Rent a donkey.

Let's go, my friend.
Let's go so you will be purified like soul.

Fly after the prey. After all,
You are not worse than a bow and arrow.

It doesn't matter whether you are rich or poor.
Sustenance has been hidden in the movement.
Come on, let's go.

You take a trip to the land of absence every night,
But when morning comes you are born again.

71.

Verse 842

Get up. The cupbearer came.
The Beauty who has been soul
To thousands of charmers came.

Clean, pure wine came. After that,
Walnuts came, honey and sugar came.

The soul came. That world came.
After that, hundreds of souls and universes
Came in different shapes.

Musk came to serve the hair
That is on top of that beauty.

He knocked at the circle of black, musky hair
And said, "Your slave, ambergris, came, ambergris."

How can I describe the sparks of your ruby lips?
What can I say to those lips?
They are better than ruby and agates.

My living has been adorned, beautified and greened
Because of that cloud-like, hyacinth hair.

Serve me new, raw wine. Look and see.
Another immature one came to the assembly.
He became our guest.

Bring that red flag
That made joyful armies victorious.

Page 14 of original Divan, Volume II.

Every difficulty and trouble
Is facilitated by Him.

Offer wine. The beginning of words has been lost.
Words are like a ship's anchor.

72.

Verse 853

My day came to say, to my night,
"May it soon be passed."
My soul came to visit my lips.

Sky listened to my *O God! O God!* so much
That, in the end, sky also started saying, "O God!"

The beloved suddenly came
With the glass full of the wine
That is forbidden by religious sects.

I used to get drunk from the first sip every time.
This time he offered the glass full to the rim.

Everyone was absolutely bewildered
By his drunkenness.
Yet, most amazing is that he became bewildered.

The sun is an ordinary star
In whichever sky his moon shines.

After seeing him riding his horse,
The new moon turned into a horseshoe.

He became soul. Earth was his body.
Isn't that glory enough for this world?

How lucky and happy is this heart
That his close friend came and united with him.

The world is full of dust and dirt.
It became beautiful, nice and decent
With the light of soul.

Every fruit ripens when its time comes.
Every work has been well harmonized.

Enough. Be silent. The one who talks with silence
Is better in front of the one who talks too much.

Be silent. That bride of soul has been tormented
For flirting with the non-confidant.

I don't find this explanation to be enough,
Because I have experience.
This rose marmalade is very nice for lovers.

I don't find this explanation to be enough
In spite of the blindness of the person
Who falls in doubt on the way of faith.

"When you are free, labor,"[58] the verse came.
He keeps pulling us. No need for words. Be silent.

But even to talk is nothing but God's draw,
Because, "He is nearer to him
Than his jugular vein."[59]

73.

Verse 870

The one who doesn't have
A trace of You is not engaging,
Even if he becomes the sun.

We are stranded, petrified at the door
And roof of love, confused and bewildered.
It is such a roof that it has no ladder.

Heart resembles a harp.
Love is a plectrum.
Why doesn't this heart scream?

Hear the yells of lovers today.
It doesn't harm you.

Every particle is full of yells and screams.
But what else could they do?
They have no tongues.

The language of particle is movement.
They have no other expression.

Hearts keep looking everywhere to see You,
But what they surmise
Doesn't even come close
To the place where you are.

There are boundaries in this world.
But my love and Yours have no boundary.

I haven't seen anything like Your spectre;
It gives kisses, but doesn't have a mouth.

Neither have I seen anything like
The looks you give;
They throw arrows but have no bow.

You gave me a belt to put on my waist,
But my heart, that resembles a child,
Doesn't have a waist.

You called and said, "Come. Reach me."
Without Your favor soul doesn't have the power
To come and reach You.

74.

Verse 882

𝓤ntidiness comes from being double-faced.
Happiness is from union.

If you are coy, the beloved will also be coy.
Two who are coy causes separation.

But if you keep begging, pleading,
Hundreds of unions, embracements come.

Coyness makes a big town smaller.
The heart that is squeezed there
Desires to travel to a far away country.

If you don't shed the blood of boasting,
That blood will rise and drown you.

Go ahead, purify this turbid coyness,
Because joy comes from cleanliness and purity.

Friends want to have pleasure,
Because desire also comes from pleasure.

He is the beloved. Don't break him.
He is not a staff. If you break him,
A sound like *crat* comes.

We know that sound of *crat* comes
From our staff, comes from separation.

75.

Verse 891

$\mathcal{B}$e pleasant.
The one who knows the secret
Knows that you are well.
He is also in pleasure.

Be as sweet as sugar. Be grateful.
The one who gives thanks will receive sugar.

Hands and pockets of thanks are filled with sugar
In order to scatter on the heads of the thankful.

If you drink his pain and smile,
You won't have any grief in your soul.

"How am I? Am I nice?" you are asking.
You would be offended if I said,
"Your face is a little bit sour."

Don't hide," you say, "but speak
In my ear so nobody else can hear."

There is no earring of loyalty in your ears.
My words will spread from your ear to others.

76.

*H*eart cries together with the Beloved's heart.
The one who talks in silence talks like that.

I would say something,
But even my tongue won't move
Because jealousy's ear is everywhere.

I know that tongue and ears are both informers.
I should tell things to the heart.
Heart is the most secure one.

There are hundreds of sparks of fire
In my eyes because of those fiery words
That come from the heart.

The most amazing thing is that there
Are so many roses, cypress and jasmines
Inside of the fire.

In order to have fire and water
Live together and walk together,
The garden and meadow grow with that fire.

O soul, you made a home
At such a garden and meadow
That heart and mind are nourished from there.

How could it be that *we* and *I* and *such and such*
Fit in that place where belief and unbelief
Cannot be squeezed in?

77.

Verse 906

We have gone. Best wishes to the rest.
Those born here always die on this planet.

The One who lives above
Knows that falling rock will surely hit the ground.

Don't be so angry. Relax. Under the earth
Masters and pupils are all the same.

O pretty one, don't be spoiled.
All the beauties buried here
Have already turned to dust.

How long do you think it stands;
This house built only by wind?

If we were bad, we died with our badness.
If we were good, we are remembered
By our goodness.

Even if you thought
You were the master of your life,
You went, just like the others.

Make good deeds your children
So as not to vanish and be forgotten.

Strings spun out of virtues remain
As the texture of the house of eternity.

The thing that stays immortal
Is that filtered, pure essence of love.

Look at the sand, how it comes and goes,
Moving endlessly, destroying one world now
And creating new ones immediately.

Page 15 of original Divan, Volume II.

Here I, at this barren land
Stand like Noah's ark.
The flood is my time of death.

Noah's ark was also waiting for waves
At the land of absence.

I laid down and slept among the silent ones,
But our voices and screams
Have long passed the boundaries.

78.

Verse 920

O greatest beloved! O beautiful
Who is best in every business,
You are deceitful, but the one
Who loves you is also deceitful.

You are the last day of judgment;
The town and bazaar have been
Turned upside-down because of you.

O beloved, loved ones are crying
Because of your love. I wouldn't even tell
About the cries of lovers.

When the time comes for me to die,
Don't watch my grave.

If you want to be resurrected,
Put me in the wind of union.

Life and joy have no value without you.
Where are you? Where are we?

If one of my blood vessels had a right mind,
Without you, my main artery would be torn.

The road appeared to me short and straight before,
Yet, there were hundreds of traps there.

I became drunk from your face
That resembles a rose garden.
I stepped on thorns. I touched the thorns.

I run to your bait like a bird, then I see
That my wings and beak are in blood.

But the irony is that the wounds you inflict on me
Are better and sweeter
Than every grain in the barn.

O my beauty, life is haram[60] without you.
Fate doesn't wake up without you.

As a matter of fact, fate is you. Life is you.
The rest are empty words, names and bruises.

O one who took me out of his heart,
You have forgotten me.
Why don't you remember me?

Once the water flows through the creek,
How does the firmament bring it back?

Be silent. The teacher of love, who tells secrets,
Keeps increasing fights and obstinacy.

79.

Verse 936

H ow come stars all around the sky
Get a hold on the sign of such a moon?

He cares for neither the believer
Nor the unbeliever; for him acknowledgment
Is the same as denial.

Has anybody ever seen a heart
That doesn't have heart?
Or an annihilated soul
That comes back to life with a sword?

If nobody has seen that, I have.
It showed its face to me.

My deeds, my knowledge are all His.
I am tired of other knowledge and worship.

That moon has stolen my sleep at night,
But has offered me union, an awake destiny.

This union is better than a thousand sleeps.
Don't even mention sleep.

A baby doesn't know what kind of effect
His crying has on the heart.

When he cries, milk flows for him
From a hundred different sources, secretly.

Cry even if you don't know why,
Because heaven is set by your cries.
Rivers will flow from your cry.

Enjoy the state of your sultanate tonight.
Watch your glory. The sultan is in
Our village tonight; so is the commander.

That morning of purity, that God's lion[61]
Who attacks, turning and forwarding,
Doesn't sleep and doesn't rest tonight.

80.

O brother, is there anything better
Than selling figs to the fig seller?

Cupbearer, remember our love.
Pleasure and joy are not good

We don't have a mind to think about work
And the store. O soul's cupbearer,
Where is the glass?

Give the glass to us. Don't leave us.
Good deeds are done quickly. Don't delay.

O One who gives life to hundreds of frustrated ones,
Don't look too hard for loyalty,
And don't reprimand us too much.

Wheat is wheat wherever it exists.
Even on the day of threshing grain,
It is still wheat for you.

If someone is a goldsmith, wherever he goes
He asks for the goldsmith.

Good people drink wine
Under the cloud full of wine.

Does your heart deem it proper
To put a load on a donkey
That is lean and wounded?

The world has its share in Your glass.
Earth becomes green with that.

Let a poor, lean one be nourished
In Your garden of mercy.

O cupbearer, don't delay
And don't decrease the wine.
Offer one glass after the other,
O One who makes our life longer.

What would soul be under the shade of the Beloved?
It would be like a fish in the river of Kevser.

Wash our fears with the clean cup of wine.
Make them pure and clean.

Don't drive us away. Even if you do,
We'll come back to your hand like a pigeon.

There is an early dawn of ten nights[63]
In your river of overflowing, foaming wine.

Come to your senses.
Shihabeddin Osmon[64] has arrived.
Tell our gazel again.

81.

Verse 965

Who could get tired of looking at that face?
Who could be tired of our beloved?

O charmer whose justice makes the sky green,
His favor fills the garden and meadow.

O graceful and coy ones, show your face.
We are fed up with our life without you.

Scatter a thousand batman[65] of meze
So all the poor will be filled.

There is such a meze at the assembly
Of your content that even the eyes
And stomach of prophets are filled by it.

When will fish be satiated with water?
When will people be satiated with God?

Don't rush. Don't go.
You are the secret chemistry. Don't go.
That copper will be satiated by chemistry.

There is another table besides this one.
The attained ones eat from that table
Filled with blessings.

Since my soul found the pleasure of His torment,
It has fallen in love with His suffering,
Is tired of his devotions.

Solomon became tired of splendor,
But a job is not satiated with trouble.

What kind of rule is it
That the horseshoe is put on in reverse?
Are the hungry less than satiated?

Be silent. Leave this rule.
Aren't you tired of this order?

82.

Verse 977

Night has come, but that is for others.
My night is day with the face of my beloved.

If thorns cover the whole world,
We are in a rose garden
With the help of the beloved.

If the world is prosperous or in ruin,
It doesn't matter; heart is drunk
And has fallen and been scattered
In front of the beloved.

Because to be aware of something
Is ignorance of the whole,
The important thing
Is to not be aware of anything.

83.

Verse 981

$\mathcal{I}$ told you a hundred times:
Watch the back and front.
Don't insist with rage and anger.

If you play the saz[66] of loyalty,
The organ of mercy
Strikes your plectrum nicely.

Page 16 of original Divan, Volume II.

You know very well that hard strikes
Will break the strings.

Serve wine. Don't sleep. We sleep,
And the instigator is awake. That's not nice.

I am a naive man. Keep talking and advising,
Muttering one thing after another.

Yet, the beloved's drunk eyes
Smile at my advice.

He jokes with my words saying, "How nicely
You are talking. Repeat it again,"

"If I don't accept your advice openly,
Secretly I'll be worse than you are."

He is obstinate. He doesn't care for anything.
The one who used to drink blood
Won't be persuaded with coyness.

Be silent. Don't be afraid of winter.
These jasmines are from God's garden.

Be silent. Even spring doesn't come in September.
March can't curl his mustache
To that garden of jasmine
That always stays green.

84.

Verse 992

$\mathcal{D}$on't see me as being apart.
I am very close to you.
You are next to me.
Don't separate yourself from me.

How could the house of the person
Who stays away from the builder prosper?

The eye that rejoiced with my eye
Becomes bright, sees absence and becomes drunk.

The heart where my wind blows
Turns into a rose garden filled with lights.

If they give a drop of honey,
It is a drop of honey, but has thousands of bees.

If they make you chief without me,
You will be worse than thousands
Who work at that business.

If you drink all the wine in the world
Without me, it won't warm your heart.

How can you read a letter under lightning?
How can you set an army with ants?

People are snow. The Beloved is the sun.
Even if you don't say so,
He would be seen and known.

People are ants. We are Solomon.
Be silent. Endure. Hide.

85.

O brother, is there anything better
Than to sell figs to the fig seller?

We live as drunks. We'll die as drunks,
And we run to judgment day as drunks.

If we die and become soil, the cupbearer
Who nourishes the slave and servant is with us.

His soil will get better and better
Because he is a lover.
His soil is mixed with soul's wine.

The soil grows flowers and says,
"We are drunk on this side and that side."

The great man becomes more beautiful
After he gets drunk. But soil is more
Drunk than he is.

When you become drunk, you turn into soil
And are laid down on the ground.
Your captain takes the anchor out.

The rope of our anchor has already been broken
For some time. Every piece of wood has been
Separated from every other piece on our ship.

But you are free from bonds
And saved from drowning,
Because every piece of wood is a guide for you.

How nice is the breaking down like that.
Look at it through the eyes of your mind.

86.

Verse 1012

O brother, is there anything better
Than to sell figs to the fig seller?

We have reached good fortune and kingdom.
Please offer the glass.

O beautiful-faced cupbearer!
O charmer who has reached all his wishes!

Even the sun gets its light from you.
Ca'fer[67] gained arms and wings from you.

We tasted the trouble of winter
And turned a pale yellow, like fall's garden.

Hear the verse, *God gives water from this spring,*[69]
And pour that red wine in the glass.

O clean sultan! O one who makes persons
Pure and clean, wash the plate of heart from sorrow.

You are the benefactor of everyone, but Your favors
Are much more for us than for other.

O Tuba tree,[69] happiness
Becomes double under your shade.

We are in love with the Beloved's beauty.
We have been dedicated to that love,
Gave up all our work and occupation.

The one who enters Your service
Receives the rank of sultan.

The person who is desired by the sun
Will be illuminated like the moon.

People have become sleepy and thirsty.
Give them wine. Quit talking.

Offer wine to the soul from Your stream,
So his health and happiness won't be spoiled,
His joy won't run away.

Today, sooner or later, a crowd
Is coming as guests.

We would sacrifice oxen and camel
To every brother who comes.

Which oxen deserves to be sacrificed?
Mushtula[70] from mushtucu.[71]

You also leave this camel's grudge
That carries sugar.

I said sugar. I didn't say glass.
But wine is hidden in the appetizer.
When appetizer is mentioned,
Wine is also mentioned.

I will keep silent if you don't offer a glass,
But you know what I do when I am silent.

87.

Verse 1032

The dervish has another sherbet.
He has a different mind and thought
In his head and eyes.

Another rapture comes to the Sufi
From the arch at the time of semâ.

You hear the music of appearance of sema,
Yet the dervish has another ear.

There are hundreds of saucepans boiling here;
But it is different
Than the dervish's boiling and exultation.

You are sitting next to someone you don't see.
You became drunk with another wine seller.

The dervish has been set free from the past.
He has a different day than morning and evening.

We talked with silence, like the soul.
We became admirers of another silent one.

88.

𝒴 ou are a loser," you said.
Even so, it is not your business.
"You are a heretic," you said.
That's what you think.

You said, "You are not a lion. You are a fox."
Let's suppose that we are the lowest of all dogs.

"You don't know anything about heart," you said.
O friend of my heart's soul, just ignore me.

89.

Verse 1042

$\mathcal{T}$ here is such brilliance in that red hair
That it is above eye, soul and conjecture together.

If you want to stand at the door,
Raise and tear the curtain of your self.

That fine soul became a form with eyes,
Brows and a brunette complexion.

The abstract God has manifested
As a form of the Prophet Mohammed.

His figure has no figure. His narcissus eye
Is, exactly, the day of resurrection.

If you look at the people, hundreds of doors
Are open from God to you.

When Mustafa's figure disappears,
Allah-u Ekber[72] covers the universe.

90.

Verse 1049

O one who kept sleeping
Woke up remembering the beloved;
That friend of the cave is coming. Get ready.

The one who grants mercy to people has come.
Wake up. Wake up and ask for mercy.

The one who gives souls to a thousand Jesus'
Has come.
Wake up, O one who died last year.

O cupbearer who feeds and educates his slaves,
Wake up for the sake of two or three drunks.

O one who became the remedy
For a hundred thousand sick ones,
That restless patient is here. Wake up.

O one whose favor holds the patient's hand,
Wake up. A thorn has gotten stuck in my feet.

O one whose beauty became a trap
For pure, clean souls, the poor prey
Is weak and incapable. Wake up.

Heart has turned into blood.
Blood, exalted, is boiling
Don't deem all this to be proper. Wake up.

Accept my apology if I asked you to wake up
When I was having a difficult time.

O narcissus who has fallen asleep while drunk!
O charmer whose face and cheek are beautiful,
Wake up.

Fill the cup with wine that you
And this servant of yours know.
Offer it to me. Wake up.

O friend, wake up as broken down
Before heart is broken.

91.

Verse 1061

𝔐y heart is tired from words about love.
Wake up from sleep.

O beloved, whose face resembles fire,
Don't stay away for even one moment from my fire.

My milk has boiled,
Has become blood because of you.
O lion, get in and splash with my blood.

I am resigned to my fate
Because you are inflexible like fate
And as quick as destiny.

Look and see how my heart's blood
Has been smeared on my caftan.

Don't ever look at me with anger.
Don't wake up that sleeping instigator.

Those sleepy, bloody, narcissus eyes
Appeared to be sleeping but, in fact,
They were not sleeping.

92.

Verse 1068

Wake up. Start serving morning wine.
Don't be obstinate. Offer your soul to the time.

Join the able ones.
Don't mix water into the wine.

Calling you is like wine.
Calling ourselves is like water.
We resemble a donkey's head.
You are the garden and meadow.

O sorrow, your death is in that bottle.
If you want to die, don't run away.

Self's death comes from fate.
The cause of the death of the dung beetle
Comes from the smell of ambergris.

Our assembly is like a garden, a meadow.
Roses are blooming. O cypress-statured cupbearer,
You also get up.

Such a shiny, fiery glass after that.
To feel shy, not to drink?
Since you are the cupbearer,
It is a sin not to drink.

Illuminate us like your beautiful face.
Hang grief like an enemy.

We left the gazel because it is your turn.
Come to the middle quickly
With agility and bravery.

93.

Verse 1077

We are brave, insolent revolutionaries
Who play with their lives.

It is a pity that this muddy flesh
Is the peer to our pure, clean soul.

Everybody comes from the beginning to the end.
Yet, we go from the end to the beginning.

The sultan has beaten that big drum again.
Friends, all the falcons have flown, are gone.

Don't fly to six dimensions. Fly that way.
Since that voice came and touched your heart,
Head that way.

O ailing heart, gather our belongings.
Only two or three days remain for our migration.

It doesn't matter whether you are
At the top or the bottom here.
Immortality, glory and superiority are all there.

Don't open the wings of words,
Because you fly wingless on that side.

The things of which we are talking are all shell.
Who has ever found the essence of that shell?

94.

The heart feels very good today,
Because You drank the blood
Of my heart yesterday.
May it do You good.

You showed Your moon face yesterday.
Yet, You manifest in thousands of shapes.
You hide Yourself in thousands of covers today.

Heart prostrates in front of this eye.
Soul turned into an earring for that ear.

You order, in every breath,
"Put your mind in your head."
Do you expect reason and sense
From the one who doesn't have them?

I am your shrill pipe. You are the one
Who talks through Me. I give your breath.
If you won't be exuberant, don't be exuberant.

Even the lion becomes a cat from fear of You.
Patience hides underground like a rat.

If every particle reaches ecstasy
And opens its arms,
That sun won't fit in those arms.

Since every particle turned into a sun
And wants to take you, sell yourself to him,
Even if it's not for cash.

Don't tell the rest of the poem.
We keep talking. The beloved keeps silent.
That is a pity.

But, what can I do? It is an old rule
That that sea keeps silent,
But the waves become exuberant.

95.

Verse 1096

Does the road of the one
Who doesn't care anything for this world
Look banal?
On the contrary, both worlds become a slave
And servant to that banal road.

O one who sees the world
And doesn't see the soul, look for one full breath.
The things you call *world* are nothing but soul.

The thing you call *world* is dust.
The sweeper and broom are all hidden in that dust.

The day you are broken like hashish
You will see where that torch is.

This love which is hidden and,
At the same time, obvious
Is bloodthirsty, cruel and rowdy.

When you are killed by His hand,
You will reach life. The living one
Is the one who died because of love.

This is such a love
That it is impossible to keep secret.
All the secrets of lovers are open.

If there were no love, there wouldn't be any beauty
Who gives pleasure. What a beauty that is!
Applaud. Applaud.

96.

We yell every night silently
So that our voice doesn't go to every ear.

We put the cover on the saucepan of royalty
So its smell doesn't go
To the noses of ordinary ones.

This is not from stinginess,
But his famous rose water
Is not for the rat's nest.

Night has come. People's excitement has subsided.
For us the time for exuberance is now.

This night has become so big and so valuable
That it is pushing yesterday with its arrogance.

We listened to music for awhile.
Now, we listen to the music of the ecstatic soul.

O sugar cane, your mouth is filled with sugar.
Don't complain. Don't get carried away.

O ring of the tambourine, you broke your kite.
Don't get involved
With the sky, the well and bucket.

Soul hunts the lion
And has given up rabbit hunting.

What is a rabbit? It is a lifeless figure.
The mirrors at hamam[73] are full of hunting animals.

Say little of the word of soul to shape.
Don't milk death's camel too much.

Page 18 of original Divan, Volume II.

Stay away from evil.
Try to be a friend of the night,
Because night covers his head with a scarf.

Take night in your arms
Until you reach the morning of union.

We forget to sleep with the call of the beloved
Who doesn't know sleep.

Know night as a black tent. You are with him.
Drums are beating. The messenger is yelling.

This instigation increases with every moment.
Love is much more tonight than yesterday.

What is night? It is the cover
Of the face of intention.
Blessings and bravo to that face.

Come to your senses. Start beating night's
Drum because Siyavush[74] is riding his horse.

97.

Verse 1122

Our musician is beautiful.
His harp is also beautiful.
Heart has been ruined by his melodies.

Watch and see how beautiful his face becomes
When he starts to play.
A new color comes to his skin.

If you are tired of living,
If you are depressed,
Get up and embrace him.
Put your arm around his waist.

98.

O hodja, be smart. How come you don't know
The wickedness and troubles of that rowdy one?

Don't scratch this face, of which even
The absent being is jealous, with your dirty nails.

That idol, that beauty cannot fit
Even in the imagination.
Don't try to carve idols in your imagination.

He is all idols and all idol worshippers.
What is left besides *all* and *everything?*
It is absence, nothingness.
There is nothing after that.

People neither understand that
Nor do I have permission to tell it.

This lentil is the rice of cross-eyed ones.
In fact, there is neither rice nor lentil.

The face that all faces envy is covered.
How are they able to recognize Him?

If you steal, take from the live ones.
O rascal who digs graves at night,
Steal the shroud.

It is inevitable that the one who dies
Because of fate and destiny
Is also the one who lives.

Be silent. How could the one
Who swallows opium during the day
Appreciate the evening?

99.

O friend of the love who remains
With his trouble and grief!
O, the light, the eyes of the Beloved!

O remedy of health, happiness and growth,
The medicine for the lover's weak body,

O beauty whose mercy and kingdom
Snatch the lover's heart
And take away his decision,

O friend who gives us preception as means,
As an envoy to the lover, then turns them into gifts,

You are beyond everything.
You don't care about the lover's struggle.

The reason for the lover's bitter weeping
Is his longing for you and your charm.

All the lover's work and trade
Depend on your order and desires.

The way the lover walks and ambles
Is because of your guidance.

O one whose binding and ties
Open the lover's heart,
O one whose advice
Becomes an earring to the lover's ear,

For some time, sleep hasn't found a place
On the lover's shy eyes.

For some time, appetite has gone
From the stomach of the lover
Who eats morsels.

For some time saffron has been growing
On the face of the lover
Who resembles a tulip garden.

For some time the lover's lap
Has been turned into a sea because of tears.

But all of these don't hurt
Since you are the one
Who finds a remedy for lovers
And takes care of their suffering.

You could buy hundreds of treasures
With one penny for the lover.
Then, you eventually donate this penny
To the lover.

O one who makes the words,
I become a guest to my God,[75]
An ornament of prose to the lover,

"I wouldn't create the skies
If you weren't there."
Seven layers of skies were giving
To the lover's domains.

Be silent. His grace
Praises the signs and words of the lover.

100.

Verse 1153

𝕎ake up from sleep. Put the harp in order.
Walk off with the moon-faced, rose-colored seducer.

Without patience, neither sleep passes,
Nor name and fame
Without being spoiled by shame.

Reason has torn thousands of mantles.
Manner has run thousands of miles away.

Heart and thought stand with anger.
The moon and stars are fighting.

Stars have gone to war.
The space of the universe has become smaller
Because of His separation.

Moon says, "How long will I be hanging
In the sky without His sun?"

The bazaar of existence may as well
Be destroyed without His agates.

O love who has a thousand names and fame,
O love whose glass is nice,
The one who gives inspiration to thousands of ideas,

O formless being who has been wrapped
With thousands of forms,
O one who gives shape to the Turk,
To the people of the land of Rum and Negroes,

Offer one glass of Your wine
Or give a handful of opium from Your garden.

Open the cover of the jar once more
So thousands of heroes
Will put their head to the ground.

Musicians in the sky should play melodies
Like a drunk.

The drunk should be freed from gossip
So he can be bewildered until resurrection
Like the ones who are resurrected.

101.

Verse 1166

The day you pass through my grave,
Remember this yelling, this exuberance.

O my eye, my light and brilliance,
Illuminate the inside of my grave.

Illuminate it so this quiet body of mine
Will prostrate in gratitude.

O harvest of roses, don't pass quickly.
Cover me with your beautiful fragrance
For just one short breath.

Even as you pass by, don't ever think
I am far from your window, your door.

The stone that has been put on top
Of my grave has tied my road,
But I don't care. I will come
Through the road of imagination.

Even if I have hundreds of satin shrouds,
I am still naked if I am not covered
By the dress of Your shape.

I resemble an ant digging a hole.
That's how I ascend
To the top of your palace.

I am like an ant. You are my Solomon.
Don't separate me from Your presence
For even one moment.

I become silent. You say the rest.
I am tired of telling and listening
All by myself.

O Shems of Tebriz, call me.
Your call is
The trumpet of resurrection for me.

102.

Verse 1177

$\mathcal{S}$ ince your love has burned me like aloe wood,
There is not one knot left in my existence.

Sometimes I pierced the wall of the castle
At the dome of the sky. At other times
I burned and melted the seal on the coin of the sun.

Sometimes I followed the sun like the moon.
A time came
When I became notched and decreased.
At other times I grew, became a full moon.

I have tried hundreds of times.
My heart can't get enough of You,
Has no patience waiting for You.

Why should I boast about generosity?
My generosity, hair by hair, is Your generosity.

Page 19 of original Divan, Volume II.

If I grab the silver knob of Your door,
It is not from my power.
This is Your favor and Your kindness.

If I am an enemy of the dawn, I must be bait.
If I deny Ahmed, I am malevolent.

You explanation sharpened my ears
Because I heard that great secret,
And I understood.

The torrent came and carried away the sleepers,
But I was thirsty and awake.

Even if I don't wipe out,
I shine my heart because of my leisure,
Because the order of *Be* is cleaning.

Every sin I have committed
Has turned into a good deed
Because your favor and kindness
Increased my grade.

Whether I ascend to the heights
Or stay at the bottom,
I rise to the throne with Your love.

If I keep laughing, it is from Your kindness.
If I envy, it is from Your zeal.

O One who knows the secret of my woof and warp,
I felt it sufficient to recall Shems of Tebriz.

103.

Verse 1191

$\mathfrak{I}$ am the drunk camel of my sultan.
I chew and regurgitate
Whatever passes through my throat.

My character resembles His face like a rose garden.
The things I scatter are my flowers.

I pull a sour face like the sea, but my arms
Are filled with pearls and coral.

Even if the Beloved doesn't want to meet me,
I am in love with meeting Him.
I am the friend of the cave for Him.

Although contempt is disgrace
In the eyes of the people,
This contempt is my praise.

Let this wind of the world blow away.
Because of this wind,
I am covered by dirt and dust.

104.

Verse 1197

O one who made me forget the time of my namaz,
The time of namaz has come. Rest a little bit.

O one who drinks the blood
Of hundreds of Kalender,[76]
Drinking blood is permissible for you.
Keep drinking.

O enemy of shame, disgrace, name and fame,
You love. After that is happiness

To be Your drunk, then to have hands and feet,
Craziness and insanity;
After that is to worry about daily affairs.

I will ask. Will you tell me?
Have you ever seen one
Whose heart has burned so much
But he is still raw?

It is obvious that my beloved
Is tired and bored. I keep silent,
Willingly or unwillingly.

105.

Verse 1203

O my pleasant soul! O my world!
I will wake you up from this deep sleep.

I will ask for your debt
Without hesitation, without shame.
You know I am a mean collector.

If I see dust and dirt in my heart,
I will wash it away with my tears.

O soul's rose sampling, I put you in my arms
To scatter to the assembly.

Give me a kiss. I take a toll
From the agate on this road.

For many years, I have been watching the road
Without a toll at this desert.

Since I want to collect a toll from the caravans,
I should yell like the guards at night.

The one who resides with me at home
Ran away from my screams.
My neighbor went away from my wailing.

106.

Verse 1211

We want neither gold nor silver.
We want arms and wings from Your favor.

We want to neither rule nor give orders.
We want to follow Your command.

O precious life, be our life.
We don't want week, month or year.

We are not a full moon
Such that we can follow the moon
And our stature become like a new moon.

In order to see Your image, we keep trying
To turn ourselves lighter than the image.

We have been going back and forth to the well
Like a bucket.
We want that beautiful Joseph.

We want You to pull the ear of soul
If he looks at others like an eye.

Be silent. How long will you keep talking?
We don't want khal[77] when hal[78] comes.

107.

𝔚 e are a branch of the rose tree, not grass.
We want a new accent.

We are the flower of sky's garden,
The wine and appetizer of God's assembly.

We are not a trench. We are water.
We are not a cloud. We are the moon.

We are Levh,[79] a pen, not the alphabet.
We are a sword, a flag, not an army.

We are wounded by the arrow of your eye,
And, at the same time, tied to your black hair.

108.

I saw your face that resembles spring.
I noticed that even the rose felt shame
After seeing you.

After You settled in my heart
I noticed that my heart became restless.

I have become an eye-like narcissus
Since I saw those drunk, narcissus eyes.

I should go to Love. Take shelter in Love,
Because Love is the fort to protect humans
From all troubles.

I have given up all earthly belongings
And pleasures. I choose Your love.

In fact, You are wealth and possessions.
You are the Soul of the universe.
They were all one, yet I saw thousands.

I died and was resurrected because of You
And saw the world a second time.

O player, if you are friend to a friend,
Play from that tune, *I saw the Beloved.*

Why should I look for the beloved in this town?
I have reached the favor of the Sultan of sultans.

I held him tightly in my arms and squeezed.
Then I saw the ceremony of sugar cane, squeezing.

I closed my mouth to words because I learned
To speak without numbers or alphabet.

I attempted to run, to amble on the road.
There was not even one foot that touched the road.

I don't protect my head from loss or damage.
I have seen so many heads wear a hat without a head.

Enough. The beloved is tired and bored.
I see dirt and dust on his memory.

109.

Verse 1238

My heart has been submerged in endless grief
Since I saw that peerless beauty.

"Tomorrow is the day they put up the bazaar,"
You said.
I noticed that the bazaar is also a pretext for you.

I have seen my heart turned into sweet and sour
Like the seeds of the pomegranate.

After seeing Your honey, the poisons
Of the world have become pure honey.

I have seen my soul like a beehive
With small holes because of You.

I am on fire, but in love I have seen
Only one flame of that inferno.

It is a chess board with hundreds of houses.
I have seen only two of them.

One house is filled with dreaminess.
The other with the wine of Mug's.[80]

Love has so many faces
That it makes time's head dizzy.

Page 20 of original Divan, Volume II.

At that time, I saw a shortcut,
A secret path from this side to that side.

I also discovered that reason,
Which searches for that road
And thoughts which deal with details
Are nothing but nonsense.

Mind, at the top of the treasure
That has no trace,
Is confused and keeps yelling,
"I found the track. I found the track."

He says, "In a dream I saw a nest for me
Under the wing of that stately bird.

"I saw the soul, that can hardly walk
From sorrow and grief, running in the land of heart.

"I saw the soul, who has seen them as fables,
Become a fable himself.

"I saw how he cries like Berbard and Cegaane.[81]
At the same time, he is not aware of his crying.

"Don't try to comb love's hair.
It cannot be combed with this comb."

If you sing melodies to him for hundreds of nights,
When morning comes, he says,
"I didn't even see you."

"I have seen every trouble that has no cure
Come running to the heart."

110.

Verse 1257

D on't ever call me old.
How can I be aged? How can I perish?

I am the fish of the fountain of life.
I have been submerged in the sea
Of milk and honey.

I don't drink water anywhere
But from the Beloved's ruby lips.

If His bow-like brows bend me like a bow,
I won't worry. I am a straight arrow on His bow.

Since You gave me wings, why shouldn't I fly?
You are my master. How could I die?

You throw me away from Yourself like an arrow.
Yet, I am still with You.
I cannot be separated from You.

111.

Verse 1263

 efore we came here we were a water-like torrent.
Before we go, our feet will fall in a trap and be tied.

We are check-mated
Even before we see a chess board.
We did not drink, even one drop, but we are drunk.

We are broken, scattered like the divided hair
Of beauties before going to war.

It seems as if we are the shadow of that idol
And worship to that idol
From the essence of existence.

He shows his shadow, but He is not around.
We are also like a shadow.
We are absent and, at the same time, we exist.

112.

We would come like dancing particles.
We would surrender ourselves to Your sun.

Every morning we would rise like the sun
From the east of love.

We would be involved with the wetness
And dryness of this world,
But we wouldn't become wet or dry.

We have seen so many drunks
Crying and yelling,
"O Glory, rise and shine so we become like gold."

We have ascended to the sky and reached the stars
Because of their begging and sorrow.

In order to buy a necklace
For that silver-bodied beauty,
We would become ambergris.

We tear our mantle to pieces
In order to wear that mantle with six edges.

We are getting by with the provisions
Of the road of absence.
Let's be drunk with red wine.

Even if they give the poison of the whole world,
We will change this to sugar inside of us.

We keep fighting like Sencer[82]
On the day the heroes ran away.

We drink the enemy's blood like wine,
Stand in front of the dagger.

We are among the circle of drunk lovers.
We come to the door every day
And hang like a ring at your door.

He is the one who wrote the decree of our mercy.
Why should we be afraid of death?

In God's spiritual dominion, in the land of absence,
We ride the gray horse of the sky.

We are concealed in the land of flesh,
But manifest openly in the land of love.

Shems of Tebriz is the soul of souls.
We rise together from the sign of eternity.

113.

𝒲e are the bewitching beauty
For the soul of lovers,
Not like a landlord who stays still at home.

Do you think we don't know
What you have in your heart?

Aren't we the ones
Who are the secrets in the imagination?
Aren't we the ones who cook every love?

Hearts are our pigeons.
We send them in a different direction
With every moment.

Body said to the soul, "Show me proof of that."
Soul said, "We are the facts and signs."

Pay attention to your speech. We are the words
And meaning inside of your mouth.

We take you in our arms with every breath.
We keep driving you to comfort and trouble.

We make you taste the wine that comes from earth
As long as you are bound by the elements of nature,
Fire, water and air.

After that, we wash out your mouth.
Then you arrive at some place.
We are the ones who are hidden there.

You'll understand us when we pull
Your existence and belonging to Absence.

You'll understand time when you gather
And fold up your form and shape from space.

You'll look around. You won't see time.
You'll say "We are in the land of no place."

You'll look everywhere. You won't see time.
You'll start saying,
"We are in the world of spacelessness."

Your body will be painted by your heart.
You'll get into play, saying,
"We are everywhere.
Everywhere is nothing but us."

You'll put your lips to our lips without lips
And acknowledge that we speak the same language.

This is the end
of the first half of

Bahr-i Hezec Ahrab Museddes

NOTES

1 The four Caliphs after the Prophet Mohammed.
2 Sophist: Skeptic.
3 Rustem: Strong hero in Persian mythology.
4 An old saying.
5 Yakin: Certainty.
6 This poem is written as a form of repeated
   quatrains.
7 Rustem-i Zal: Rustem's father.
8 Koran XIX-25.
9 Keykubad: Name of the just king of the
   legendary
   Key dynasty of ancient Persia. A great king.
10 Six-cornered: Six dimensions.
11 Mustafa: Prophet Mohammed.
12 Kevser: River in paradise.
13 Kadir: The 27th of Ramadan, when the Koran
   was revealed.
14 Arabic folk tale.
15 Trotter: Bone part of sheeps head.
16 Kulah: A conical hat.
17 Friend of cave, Abu Bakr. Koran IX-40.
18 Iman: Religious leader.
19 This gazel was written in Arabic.
20 Kadir's nights: The 27th of Ramadan when the
   Koran was revealed.
21 Berat: 15th of Shaban; when the Prophet
   Mohammed was given the revelation of his
   mission.
22 Suhey: The star Canopus.
23 Hatem: Proverbial man known for his
   generosity.

24   Abdal: According to Sufis, Abdal are the seven
      sages who attained divine truth after the
      Prophet Mohammed's departure.
25   Hamza: Uncle of prophet.
26   Koran LXXXIX-14.
27   Pir: Patron saint.
28   Ahmed: Prophet Mohammed.
29   Abu: The father of ignorance.
30   This gazel was said probably after Shems
      returned.
31   Verses 9-12 are in Arabic.
32   Zulfekaar: Iman Ali's sword.
33   Meze: An appetizer.
34   This verse is from Divan's Istambul University
      version.
35   Franks: European reference to the Crusaders.
36   Azer: Uncle of Abraham.
37   Old custom for women and children.
38   Taraz: City in Central Asia famous for its
      beauties.
39   Burak: White horse on which the Prophet
      ascended to heaven.
40   These quatrains are very similar to gazel 50.
41   Sahur: The meal before dawn; during Ramadan.
42   Gayb: Occult, unknown.
43   Kalender: Kalenderlik: A Sufi school.
44   Mahmud: Famous ruler of Gazne.
45   Eyaz: Mahmud's slave.
46   This verse is not in Divan's Konya version.
47   Suheyl: A star.
48   Rebab: A three-stringed violin.
49   Kebap: Roasted meat.
50   Shibli-Abu Bekr: a Sufi who died in 940.
      Abu-l hasan Harkan: Sufi who died in 1033.

51 Koran VII-172.
52 Ritual ablution.
53 Koran LXXVIII-7.
54 There is an old belief that fairies exist in baths and waterfalls.
55 Koran LIII-14. Sidre: Border tree. The Archangel Gabriel went to that tree with the Prophet.
56 This verse is from Istanbul University, not Konya.
57 Koran XII-24.
58 Koran XCIV-7.
59 Koran L-16.
60 Haram: Religiously forbidden.
61 Iman Ali-Hayderi-Kerrar.
62 Even numbered verses in this gazel are in Arabic.
63 Koran LXXXIX-2.
64 Shihabeddin Osmon: According to Eflaki-Menakub, this person is Osman-i Kavval or Osman-I Guyende. A musician of the inner circle of Mevlana.
65 Batman: Unit of weight.
66 Saz: Stringed instrument.
67 Ca'fer: Ca'fer-i Tayyar.
68 Koran LXXVI, 21.
69 Tuba: Tree in paradise.
70 Mushtula: To give good news.
71 Mushtucu: One who gives good news.
72 Allah-u Ekber: God is great.
73 Hamam: Turkish bath. Apparently they did have animal figures on the mirror there at that time.

74 Siyavush: Son of Keykaveus. (Iranian
       mythology.)
75 Hadis: Ahadisi: Mesnevi page 36.
76 Kalender: Sufi school.
77 Khal: words and speech.
78 Hal: Ecstasy.
79 Levh: Levh-i Mahfuz. The tablet of god's
       decree. Preserved to the end of time.
80 Mug: Magician, fire worshipper, tavern keeper.
81 Berbard, Cegaane: Stringed instruments.
82 Sencer: A Persian king.

Typeset in Caslon 224 Book & Duc de Berry by
Powerhouse
Los Angeles, CA

Printed & Bound by
Publishers Press
Salt Lake City, UT